DIE ALONE, THEN

The Loneliness Lie & Why Peace Outweighs Partnership

MINA V. ADLER

MINERVA DOY
PUBLISHING

Paperback ISBN: 978-1-7646443-0-3
Hardcover ISBN: 978-1-7646443-1-0
Ebook ISBN: 978-1-7646319-9-0

For Andy Standy, Tom T. and Bobbi
Alone but never lonely

"I'll only have you if you're sweeter than my solitude."
– Warsan Shire

About the Author

Mina V. Adler

Mina V. Adler writes the kinds of sentences polite society wishes women would stop saying out loud. Her work examines the quiet economics of relationships — the unpaid labor, the cultural scripts, and the emotional negotiations women are expected to perform without complaint.

With a voice that is part cultural autopsy, part stand-up monologue, Ms Adler dismantles the myth that female happiness must orbit male approval.

She is less interested in romance as fantasy than in romance as infrastructure — who benefits from it, who maintains it, and why women are finally starting to question the maintenance schedule.

She did not arrive at these ideas from theory alone. Like most women, Ms Adler has lived through the exhausting curriculum: the over-explaining, the emotional translation, the strategic softening of opinions so that a grown man does not feel threatened by basic conversation. She emerged from that experience not bitter, but observant — and with a deeply suspicious eye toward any system that tells women their peace is negotiable. Her writing blends cultural analysis with dry, unsentimental humour, the kind that appears when someone has finally stopped pretending that the emperor's emotional maturity is wearing clothes.

Ms Adler lives a life that critics of independent women often describe with great concern: she reads widely, maintains strong friendships, enjoys long stretches of uninterrupted silence, and appears alarmingly content without performing romantic distress.

When she is not writing, she can usually be found drinking coffee, watching the world with anthropological interest, and quietly disappointing anyone who believes a woman's life must revolve around securing male approval. She considers peace a perfectly acceptable life goal — and highly recommends it.

Above all, she would be supremely happy to die alone.

Die Alone, Then

The Loneliness Lie & Why Peace Outweighs Partnership

Mina V. Adler

CONTENTS

INTRODUCTION

The Threat They Think It Is

"**D**ie alone, then!"

It is sometimes shouted, but mostly delivered softly. Almost tenderly. As if the speaker is offering protection from such a terrible fate.

My inner response would be, "Don't threaten me with a good time!"

But, seriously, "You'll die alone" is not a prediction. It's a threat. It's a warning.

And it's almost always directed at women.

A man who remains unmarried is a bachelor. Eligible. Respected. Independent.

A woman who remains unmarried – the "spinster" – is a question mark. "What is wrong with her?" "What is she lacking?"

This asymmetry is not accidental. It's architecture.

From girlhood, women are trained to understand that partnership is not simply desirable — it is stabilising. It is protective. It is proof of worth.

Fairy tales do not end with the heroine securing financial literacy or building a female cooperative housing model.

They end with selection. With being *chosen.*

The cultural story is clear: *being alone is the failure state.*

But here is the unspoken truth — many women are already alone.

Alone in conversation.
Alone in responsibility.
Alone in emotional regulation.
Alone in ambition.
Alone while lying next to someone.

I was never more alone than in my marriage.

And yet, we are told the true terror lies elsewhere — in the absence of a man entirely.

The phrase "die alone" works because it conflates solitude with abandonment. It suggests that, without male partnership, a woman will be unsupported, unloved, and ultimately discarded by society. It implies vulnerability. It implies weakness. It implies that male presence equals security.

But what if that equation is flawed?

What if attachment to the wrong man is not security — but risk?

What if the real instability is binding your life to someone who depends on you emotionally in ways that erode you?

We do not talk enough about erosion.

Not dramatic heartbreak. Not betrayal. Not catastrophe.

Erosion: The slow wearing down of vitality when you are the emotional scaffolding for another adult. The gradual dulling of sharp edges. The habitual softening of opinions. The learned reflex of reassurance.

"Are you upset?"
"Are we okay?"
"Do you still love me?"
"Why are you so distant?"

Questions that do not signal intimacy — but dependency.

This book is not about villains. It is about *imbalance.*

Needy men are not always cruel. In fact, many are gentle. They are articulate. They may even be self-aware. But self-awareness without self-regulation still lands on a woman's lap.

A needy man may not shout. He may sigh.

He may not control overtly. He may subtly require.

He may not forbid your success. He may simply grow fragile in its presence.

And because women are trained to detect emotional shifts with forensic precision, we adjust.

We recalibrate our tone. We temper our ambition. We dilute our anger. We cushion our truth.

This adjustment becomes so constant that it disappears from conscious awareness.

We call it compromise. We call it love. But often, it is *management.*

The management of male insecurity has been normalized to the point that women mistake it for partnership. And when a woman grows tired of this dynamic — when she begins to imagine a life without it — she is reminded of the looming threat.

"You'll die alone."

Let us examine this carefully. Everyone dies alone. Rarely is death a group project.

What the phrase really means is this: *If you refuse to accommodate male dependency, you will be socially punished with isolation.*

That is the fear being sold. And for generations, it worked.

Historically, marriage was an economic survival strategy for women. It was not primarily about romance. It was about property rights, legitimacy, safety, access to resources. A woman without a husband often lacked legal standing. She lacked income. She lacked protection.

But we no longer live in that era.

Women own property. Women run corporations. Women build communities. Women earn. Women inherit. Women invest.

And yet the psychological script remains. The panic has simply shifted from *economic survival* to *emotional survival.*

We are told: You may have money, but who will hold you when you're sick? An important question.

But equally important: Who will care for you if you are emotionally depleted for decades because you prioritized soothing someone else over strengthening yourself? Who will hold you then?

There is a particular lie embedded in *the fear of solitude: that a woman without a man is unsupported.*

This ignores the profound infrastructure of female friendship. It ignores chosen family. It ignores siblings, colleagues, communities, extended networks. It ignores that many married women rely primarily on other women for emotional sustenance anyway.

Women do not lack connection. Women lack permission to choose peace over performance.

Let us speak plainly. Some men want partnership. Others want a regulator.

They want someone to absorb the spikes of their insecurity. Someone to affirm their desirability. Someone to translate their emotions into coherence. Someone to orbit them gently enough that they never feel irrelevant.

This is not masculinity. This is dependency. And dependency, when disguised as love, is extraordinarily draining.

Women are socialized to be attuned. We notice shifts in breathing. We register silence. We feel temperature changes in a room before they are articulated. This attunement is a strength — until it becomes a leash.

When you are partnered with a needy man, your nervous system never fully rests. You are listening. Monitoring. Adjusting.

And over time, your own interior voice grows faint.

The first night alone after leaving such a dynamic can be disorienting. There is no one to check on. No one to reassure. No one to anticipate.

The quiet can feel foreign.

Then something unexpected happens.

Your body relaxes. Not because you do not care — but because you are no longer on call.

This is the beginning of a dangerous realisation: *Peace feels better than proximity.*

This realisation is destabilising — not just personally, but culturally. Because if women collectively decide that peace outranks partnership, entire systems shift. Consumption shifts. Housing shifts. Power shifts. Birth rates shift. Economic leverage shifts.

A woman who is not afraid of being alone cannot be pressured easily.

She negotiates differently. She dates differently. She invests differently. She votes differently. And, when standards are not met, she leaves.

This is why the threat persists.

"Die alone" is not about death. It is about *deterrence.*

It is about keeping women available for emotional labor.

Let us define emotional labor clearly: the unpaid, often invisible work of managing another person's feelings to maintain relational harmony.

Women have performed this labor so consistently that it is assumed to be innate. But it is learned. Conditioned. Rewarded.

A "good woman" anticipates needs. She soothes conflict. She does not destabilise male ego.

A peaceful woman, however, is less accommodating. She does not rush to reassure, nor apologise for ambition. She does not translate her anger into softness, nor accept chronic neediness as romance.

And because of this, she is called difficult.

The accusation of difficulty is often a sign that a woman has stopped performing.

This book is not anti-love. It is *anti-imbalance.*

There are men capable of partnership that enhances peace rather than consumes it. They exist. But they are not entitled to women's endurance while they mature.

A woman is not a rehabilitation centre.

If a relationship multiplies your stability, your joy, your clarity — it is an asset. If it requires continuous emotional management to remain functional — it is a liability.

The question is **not**: Will I die alone?

The question is: *How do I want to live?*

There are women who remain in exhausting partnerships because the social validation feels safer than the unknown. They attend weddings together. They post curated photographs. They host dinners. They appear aligned.

But privately, they are tired. Tired of explaining basic empathy. Tired of buffering ego. Tired of shrinking success. Tired of being the stronger one.

There is nothing noble about permanent exhaustion. There is nothing romantic about imbalance. There is nothing tragic about choosing peace.

If solitude frightens you, *examine the source of that fear.* Is it genuine loneliness — or *anticipated judgment?*

Most women are not terrified of their own company. *They are terrified of being perceived as unwanted.*

But unwanted by whom?

By men who require constant affirmation? By institutions that depend on female accommodation? By a culture that equates female worth with relational status?

There is a different life available. A life where evenings are quiet by choice. Where finances are structured for autonomy. Where friendships are deep and reciprocalWhere sexual intimacy is selected, not obligated. Where silence is restorative, not tense. Where ambition does not need to be dimmed to protect someone else's comfort.

This is not isolation. It is *sovereignty.*

And sovereignty unsettles those who benefit from your compliance.

If, at the end of your life, you are surrounded by friends, siblings, colleagues, nieces, students, collaborators — but not a husband — have you died alone? Or have you lived fully?

The phrase collapses complexity into shame. We will expand it back into truth.

You may die alone. You may not. But you will live every day before that moment.

The real decision is not about the final hour. It is about the decades leading to it. Will they be spent negotiating your own diminishment? Or will they be spent at peace?

This book is for the woman who is beginning to suspect that calm is more intoxicating than chaos. For the woman who feels relief when she imagines no longer managing someone. For the woman who has been warned — and is no longer persuaded.

If peace costs you a relationship that required you to disappear, that is not loss.

That is reclamation.

And if choosing peace evokes the "Die alone, then!" threat — Smile.

And live well first.

PART I: THE LIE

How Women Have Been Taught to Fear Their Own Freedom

Chapter 1

THE MYTH OF FEMALE INCOMPLETENESS

(Or, The Greatest Marketing Campaign Ever Sold to Women)

- The historical marketing of marriage.

- Religion, romance, economics.

- Why "happily ever after" required unpaid labor.

"Lower your standards or you'll die alone."

This chapter dismantles the oldest scare tactic in the book. Where it came from, why it's aimed almost exclusively at women, and how fear has been used as social control. The myth that partnership is survival, and singlehood is failure.

Let us begin with a dangerous sentence: Women were never incomplete.

They were told (and believed) they were. There is a difference.

For thousands of years, the most profitable fiction ever sold to women was not that diamonds are romantic or that youth is currency.

It was this: **Without a man, you are unfinished**.

That belief did not emerge naturally from female biology. It was engineered. Reinforced. Polished. Passed down through religion, law, literature, economics, and eventually cinema.

It is not instinct. It is architecture. And it has held remarkably well.

Step One: Create the Problem

Every successful marketing campaign begins by creating a problem that does not organically exist.

Women, left alone, have always been capable. Historically, they farmed, traded, midwifed, healed, managed households, raised children, built networks. They survived wars. Famines. Plagues. They were not fragile creatures waiting for rescue.

But competence is inconvenient when you need compliance.

So the narrative shifted.

Instead of presenting women as capable but constrained by law, society reframed them as naturally incomplete. Their primary identity was redefined relationally. Daughter. Wife. Mother.

Notice what disappears in that sequence. **Self**.

If your identity is always relational, then independence feels unnatural. You are defined by attachment. And if attachment defines you, then detachment threatens you.

Thus the myth was born: **a woman alone is a problem to be solved**.

Marriage Was Never About Love

Before romance, before poetry, before white dresses and diamond rings, marriage was property management. It was alliance-building. It was inheritance insurance. It was a transfer of economic control.

Women were currency in these arrangements. They were not naive about this. Everyone knew it.

But as societies evolved and overt ownership of women became less socially acceptable, marriage required rebranding.

You cannot openly tell half the population that their primary function is labor and reproduction. That model eventually collapses.

So the sales pitch softened. Marriage became love. Love became destiny. Destiny became identity.

This was not evolution. It was strategy. Because if women believed marriage was their deepest desire, they would pursue it voluntarily. And voluntary compliance is far more stable than forced obedience.

Religion: Sanctifying Dependency

Religion did not invent female dependency — but it sanctified it.

Across traditions, the structure was similar: men led; women followed. Men interpreted; women obeyed. Men held authority; women upheld virtue.

A woman's highest calling was framed as service — to God through husband, to husband through submission, to children through sacrifice.

Holiness was not self-actualisation. It was self-erasure.

A woman outside marriage was often treated with suspicion. Why had she not been chosen? Was she undesirable? Difficult? Spiritually lacking?

Even when celibacy was praised, it was praised only if directed toward religious devotion — another form of service.

The possibility that a woman might choose solitude simply because she preferred peace was not considered. Because peace without permission is rebellion. And rebellion must be discouraged.

Religion did not need to threaten women overtly. It simply equated obedience with virtue. And women, eager to be good, complied.

Romance: The Velvet Cage

Religion enforced the structure. Romance made it seductive.

Romantic love was the velvet cage — soft enough to feel luxurious, sturdy enough to contain. Suddenly, marriage was not duty. It was longing. Not obligation — fulfillment.

The romantic heroine did not marry because she must. She married because she desired. And desire is powerful.

The genius of romantic propaganda is that it disguises sacrifice as transcendence. The woman who gives up her ambition? She has chosen love. The woman who tolerates volatility? She believes in passion. The woman who forgives repeatedly? She understands him.

Romantic narratives taught women that intensity equals depth. That drama equals devotion. That emotional turbulence equals destiny.

But what was rarely depicted? Boredom. Resentment. Unequal labor. Exhaustion. Those do not photograph well.

So the story ends at the kiss. Not at the sink full of dishes. Not at the third argument about responsibility. Not at the quiet grief of shrinking yourself to maintain harmony.

Romance sells the beginning. Women live the aftermath.

The Economics No One Mentions

Strip away the poetry, and economics remains.

Marriage has always depended on female labor. Cooking. Cleaning. Childcare. Emotional management. Social coordination. Sexual availability. Elder care.

For centuries, this labor was uncompensated and expected. It still largely is. Even today, in dual-income households, women disproportionately manage domestic logistics and emotional climate.

The difference now? They also work full-time.

Marriage adapted beautifully to women's economic independence. It did not collapse. It simply expanded expectations.

Women were told they could "have it all."

What they were not told was that "all" meant **doing it all.** Career and caregiving. Ambition and accommodation. Leadership at work, deference at home.

And if they faltered? Personal failure. Not systemic imbalance.

The myth of incompleteness ensures participation in this arrangement. Because if you believe marriage completes you, then the labor inside it feels meaningful rather than exploitative.

You endure. You rationalize. You minimize. You tell yourself this is normal.

The Fear Machine

Why does the myth persist?

Fear.

Fear is extraordinarily effective. "You'll end up alone." "Your biological clock is ticking." "No one wants an older woman." "You're too independent." "Men don't like that."

These messages are not random. They are corrective tools. They are designed to redirect women back toward relational urgency.

A woman who is afraid of being alone will tolerate more. She will rush decisions. She will accept mediocrity. She will confuse attention with compatibility.

Fear lowers standards. And lowered standards maintain supply.

The Manufactured Deadline

One of the most powerful tools in the myth of incompleteness is the deadline.

Women are told their desirability has an expiration date. Youth is framed as currency. Marriage becomes a race. The clock ticks. Urgency intensifies.

The subtext is clear: secure a man before you lose leverage.

This urgency distorts discernment. It encourages settling. It rewards endurance over evaluation.

And once married, the same system that rushed women into partnership offers little support when imbalance emerges.

The clock served its purpose. You signed up. Now, manage.

Why Wholeness Is Threatening

A woman who believes she is whole negotiates differently. She does not pursue partnership as proof. She does not interpret singleness as deficiency. She does not panic at solitude.

She evaluates compatibility with calm. And calm is destabilising to systems built on urgency.

If women stopped fearing incompleteness, marriage rates would not necessarily collapse — but they would transform.

Partnership would need to compete with peace.

That is a high bar. And many men have not been socialized to meet it. Because historically, they did not need to.

The Quiet Reality Women Rarely Admit

Many women in long-term relationships experience something they struggle to articulate. Not hatred. Not betrayal.

They experience **fatigue**, which leads to jadedness or resentment.

The fatigue of being the emotionally literate one. The organizer. The smoother. The anticipator. The manager.

This fatigue is often invisible even to themselves. They believe it is simply adulthood. Responsibility.

But when they imagine living alone — just for a moment — something shifts. Their body relaxes. Not because they do not love their partner. But because they are tired of carrying.

The myth of incompleteness tells them that this relief is selfish. That longing for quiet is failure. That wanting less emotional responsibility is cold.

But what if it is **clarity**?

The Lie of Female Destiny
The final layer of propaganda is destiny.

"You were meant to find someone." "Women are wired for connection." "Everyone needs a partner."

Connection is human. Dependency is optional. The conflation of the two has trapped generations.

Women are social creatures. So are men.

But men are not told their humanity is invalid without romantic attachment. Women are.

A man alone is independent. A woman alone is suspicious. Or somehow lacking. Or a man-hater. Or a lesbian.

Why? Because a woman who centers herself disrupts the script.

She may invest in friendships. She may build wealth. She may travel. She may rest. She may create.

She may choose lovers without offering lifelong service.

She may decide that peace is preferable to partnership.

This possibility undermines the mythology.

So the mythology fights back.

The Most Radical Realisation

The most radical realisation a woman can have is this:

I was never incomplete. I was conditioned to believe I was.

And once that conditioning cracks, everything changes.

She stops chasing validation. She stops fearing age. She stops tolerating imbalance. She stops apologising for standards. She stops interpreting solitude as punishment.

She begins asking a different question. Not "Who will choose me?" But "Do I choose this?"

That shift is seismic. It redistributes power. It changes negotiations. It transforms dating from pursuit to assessment. It reframes marriage from necessity to option.

And options destabilize systems built on obligation.

What Happens When the Spell Breaks

When a woman no longer believes she is incomplete, the fear loses leverage. The warnings sound hollow. The urgency fades. The clock becomes background noise.

She may still desire partnership. But she will not pursue it at the cost of self. She will not confuse attention with compatibility. She will not mistake neediness for intimacy. She will not romanticize imbalance.

And if partnership does not enhance her peace, she will walk. Not angrily. Not theatrically. But calmly.

And calm refusal is far more powerful than dramatic rebellion. Because it cannot be shamed.

The Truth That Terrifies Systems

Here is what terrifies systems that rely on female incompleteness:

A woman who believes she is whole does not beg. She does not cling. She does not negotiate from fear. She does not tolerate chronic emotional dependency. She does not need a man to validate her existence.

She chooses. And choice is power.

The myth of female incompleteness was never about romance. It was about control. It ensured labor. It ensured compliance. It ensured continuity.

But myths weaken when exposed.

And once you see the architecture, you cannot unsee it. Marriage may still be beautiful. Love may still be profound. Partnership may still be deeply fulfilling.

But none of it completes you. You were complete before it.

And if it demands your diminishment to sustain itself, it is not fulfillment. It is extraction.

The most dangerous woman in any system is not the loudest. It is the one who knows she was never lacking. The one who no longer fears solitude. The one who understands that wholeness is not bestowed.

It is remembered. And once remembered, it cannot be revoked.

Chapter 2

THE LONELINESS LIE

- Manufactured deadlines

- Ridicule for the solitary woman

- Alone does not mean lonely

They told you it would be unbearable.

That if you did not secure a man, you would sit in a silent house, watching the light fade, glued to RomComs, consumed by regret.

They told you the clock was ticking. That companionship is oxygen. That partnership is safety. That a woman alone is a woman failed.

They did not tell you about the other loneliness. The loneliness of lying next to someone who does not see you. The loneliness of explaining yourself for the hundredth time. The loneliness of dimming, soothing, managing, shrinking. The loneliness of being needed but not known.

They warned you about solitude.

They never warned you about containment.

And so you fear the wrong thing.

The Social Construction of Panic
From childhood, the narrative is clear: A girl's story culminates in coupling.

The movies end at the wedding. The songs crescendo at commitment. The fairy tales close when the prince arrives.

No one writes ballads about a woman who chose peace. No one builds industries around celebrating female solitude.

But entire markets depend on your fear of it. Dating apps monetize it. Wedding industries inflate it. Self-help empires exploit it. Even well-meaning relatives reinforce it.

"Don't leave it too late." "You don't want to be alone." "Men prefer younger women." "You don't want to be left on the shelf."

The implication is constant: Partnership is proof of worth. Without it, you are unfinished.

And fear is a powerful motivator.

The Manufactured Deadline
The "clock" is invoked like a curse.

You are reminded of your age as though it is a moral failing.

Twenty-five: hopeful. Thirty: urgent. Thirty-five: concerning. Forty: tragic. Fifty: Spinster

Men age into gravitas. Women age into warnings.

The message is not subtle: Settle now or suffer later.

So you rush. You compromise. You rationalize. You overlook incompatibilities because the alternative feels catastrophic.

But catastrophic to whom? To you? Or to a culture that does not know what to do with a woman who opts out?

Alone vs. Unsupported

There is a distinction no one bothers to clarify: Alone is physical. Unsupported is relational.

You can be single and deeply supported. By friends. By community. By purpose. By yourself.

You can be partnered and profoundly unsupported. By a man who dismisses your feelings. Who resents your growth. Who requires your management. Who does not protect your peace.

Which is lonelier? A quiet Sunday in your own apartment, reading, unbothered? Or a Sunday spent negotiating a mood you did not create?

Which feels heavier? Cooking dinner for yourself in calm silence? Or cooking dinner while calculating how to avoid triggering tension?

We have conflated physical proximity with emotional nourishment. They are not the same.

The Statistics They Don't Lead With

Studies consistently show that single women without children often report high life satisfaction.

Married men live longer than single men.

Married women? The data is less glowing.

Women in unequal marriages experience higher stress levels. Higher rates of anxiety. Greater emotional load.

Men benefit disproportionately from marriage. They gain emotional support. Health monitoring. Social stability. Domestic organization.

Women often gain more work.

Yet the cultural panic remains targeted at women.

Why? Because a woman who does not fear loneliness is difficult to control.

The Myth of the Crazy Cat Lady

The caricature is cruel: A solitary woman with too many cats, too much bitterness, too little love. She is the punchline.

But what if she is peaceful? What if she reads at night without interruption? What if she travels spontaneously? What if she makes decisions without negotiation? What if she rests?

The ridicule serves a purpose. It reinforces the narrative that female independence is pathetic. It discourages defection.

If women believed solitude could be rich, many would reconsider what they tolerate.

So the myth persists.

Better to mock her than to examine her contentment.

The Quiet Home

Let us imagine it honestly.

You come home. There is no one there. No shoes in the hallway. No television blaring. No tension humming beneath the surface. No man asking, "What are we having for dinner?"

Just space.

You cook what you want. You eat when you want. Or not at all – if you want. You go to bed when you want. You speak without filtering.

Is it always blissful? No. There are moments of ache. Humans are social creatures.

But ache is not the same as erosion.

Loneliness comes in waves. But chronic self-abandonment is a tide that never recedes.

The quiet house is not the horror story you were promised. For many women, it is relief.

The Emotional Mirage of Partnership

You were told partnership equals intimacy.

But intimacy requires mutual exposure. How intimate is a relationship where you self-edit? How intimate is a relationship where your ambition is softened? How intimate is a relationship where you manage his moods?

Closeness without equality is not intimacy. It is proximity.

You can share a bed and still feel unknown. You can share finances and still feel unseen. You can share a surname and still feel separate.

The loneliness lie equates proximity with fulfillment. But fulfillment requires reciprocity.

Fear as Social Glue

Fear keeps systems intact.

If women were not afraid of being alone, the standards would rise overnight.

If women believed peace was preferable to unequal partnership, many relationships would dissolve.

If women stopped tolerating emotional immaturity, men would be forced to grow or lose access.

So fear is reinforced. Through jokes. Through warnings. Through subtle pity for the unmarried: "You'll find someone." "Don't give up." "It will happen when you least expect it."

As if partnership is the ultimate prize. As if solitude is a holding pattern.

As if your life has not already begun.

The Women Who Walk Away

There is a growing demographic. Women who have left marriages. Women who have chosen not to marry. Women who have ended long-term relationships without immediate replacement.

They are not collapsing. They are building. Careers. Friendships. Homes. Peace.

They are discovering something dangerous: Life does not end without a man. It expands differently.

And once that knowledge spreads, the bargaining power shifts.

"But don't you get lonely?" Yes. Sometimes.

Loneliness is part of the human condition. But so is frustration. So is disappointment. So is resentment.

The question is not whether you will feel lonely. The question is which loneliness you prefer. The acute pang of missing companionship? Or the dull ache of being misunderstood? The occasional empty Friday night? Or the daily negotiation of your own boundaries?

Loneliness in solitude is clean.

Loneliness in partnership is confusing. Because you cannot point to absence. The person is right there. And yet something essential is missing.

Loneliness in a relationship, as in a crowd, is the most cutting loneliness of all.

The Economics of Peace

Peace has value.

Sleep without bracing. Money spent without negotiation. Time used without explanation.

You underestimate the cost of constant compromise. You underestimate the energy required to maintain harmony. You underestimate the toll of anticipating moods.

When women leave unequal relationships, many report the same sensation: Lightness.

Not because they hate men. Because the invisible labor stops. The silence becomes restorative rather than tense. The home becomes sanctuary rather than workplace.

Peace is not empty. It is spacious.

The Cultural Backlash

As more women opt out, backlash intensifies. They are called selfish. Unrealistic. Too picky. Career-obsessed. Man-hating.

The narrative shifts from pity to accusation. If she cannot be shamed into coupling, she must be villainized.

But standards are not cruelty. Refusal is not hatred. Desiring equality is not extremism.

The backlash reveals the truth: Autonomous women disrupt expectations.

Reframing the Question

Instead of asking, "What if I end up alone?" Ask: What if I end up exhausted? What if I end up resentful? What if I end up smaller? What if I spend decades managing someone else's emotional world? What if I abandon myself to avoid temporary solitude?

Which outcome terrifies you more?

Because you have been trained to fear the wrong one.

The False Urgency

Urgency drives poor decisions.

When you believe time is running out, you accept what you would otherwise reject. You reinterpret red flags as quirks. You excuse immaturity as growth potential. You tell yourself you can adapt.

But adaptation has limits. And the urgency was often exaggerated.

Partnership is not scarce. Compatible partnership is rarer. There is a difference.

Better no partner than misaligned partnership. Better patience than permanent compromise.

The Expansion of Female Networks

Something else is happening quietly. Women are building rich social ecosystems. Deep friendships. Intentional communities. Professional networks. Chosen families.

The myth that only romantic partnership prevents loneliness is collapsing.

Connection does not require marriage. Intimacy does not require cohabitation. Support does not require a husband.

The more women invest in diversified connection, the less power the loneliness lie holds.

When Partnership Is Worth It

This book is not an argument against love. It is an argument against fear-based coupling.

Partnership is beautiful when it is equal. When your growth is celebrated. When your peace is protected. When emotional labor is shared. When ambition is admired. When opinions are respected.

In such partnership, solitude loses appeal. Because the relationship amplifies you.

But unequal partnership drains you. And no ring compensates for depletion.

The Courage to Wait

Waiting is uncomfortable. It requires trust in your own value. It requires resisting cultural panic. It requires tolerating questions at family gatherings. It requires confronting your own fear honestly.

But courage is not absence of fear. It is refusal to be governed by it.

If you are partnered, let it be because it enhances you. If you are single, let it be because you will not settle. Both positions can be powerful. Neither requires shame.

The Moment of Clarity

There is often a moment. A quiet one. When you realize *you are more afraid of losing yourself than losing him.*

That moment changes everything.

The loneliness lie weakens. Because you understand something profound: You are not half of anything. You are whole.

Partnership is an addition, not a completion. And addition should increase value. Not dilute it.

The Radical Conclusion

Imagine a generation of women who are not afraid to be alone. Who do not rush. Who do not shrink. Who do not subsidize immaturity.

What would men have to become? Stronger. Kinder. More self-aware. More emotionally literate.

The loneliness lie does not only hurt women. It stunts men. Because as long as women fear solitude more than inequality, men have little incentive to evolve.

But when fear dissolves, standards rise. And everyone grows.

Final Truth

You were told: Better a flawed partnership than none. Better company than quiet. Better compromise than solitude.

But here is the truth: Better peace than proximity. Better integrity than urgency. Better wholeness than attachment born of fear.

You are not running out of time. You are running toward clarity. And clarity is louder than panic.

If loneliness visits, greet it. It will not stay forever.

But if self-abandonment moves in, it will unpack its bags.

Choose wisely which guest you tolerate.

Peace, dear reader, is not a consolation prize. It is the standard. And once you internalize that, the lie collapses.

Chapter 3

The Social Threat of the Unattached Woman

- Spinster panic.

- Why independent women destabilize systems.

- Cultural suspicion of women who don't center men.

There is a particular discomfort that arises when a woman says, calmly and without bitterness:

"I'm not looking."

Not divorced and devastated. Not heartbroken and healing. Not "taking a break."

Just — not looking.

The reaction is immediate and involuntary. The air tightens. Faces rearrange themselves into concern. Advice rushes in uninvited. Jokes appear, thinly disguised warnings follow. Sometimes pity. Sometimes irritation. Occasionally hostility.

Because a woman unattached by circumstance is one thing.

A woman unattached by choice is another.

She unsettles people. Not because she is loud. Not because she is angry. But because she is self-contained.

And self-contained women have always been dangerous.

Attachment as Social Infrastructure

For centuries, societies have relied on women's attachment to men as a stabilising mechanism. Marriage was never merely personal. It was structural.

It organized property. It regulated inheritance. It managed sexuality. It assigned labour. It ensured continuity.

Most importantly, it ensured that women's labour — reproductive, domestic, emotional — remained predictable and *accessible*.

Marriage was not simply a romantic union. It was an administrative solution.

An unattached woman disrupts that solution.

She introduces unpredictability into systems that depend on women being legible, assignable, and anchored to men. And systems, like all bureaucracies, loathe unpredictability.

The discomfort people feel around unattached women is not emotional. It is structural. She represents a variable that cannot be easily managed.

The Invention of Spinster Panic

The word "spinster" did not begin as an insult. It was an occupation. A woman who spun yarn. A woman who worked. A woman who earned.

She was not idle. She was not pitiable. She was not defective. She was self-sufficient. Most threateningly, she was economically independent.

And that was the problem. As societies increasingly defined women not by contribution but by relation, independence became suspect. The unmarried woman no longer fit neatly into the relational order. She could not be categorized as wife. She was not under the governance of a husband. Her labour was not automatically allocated.

So her identity was rewritten.

The spinster became lonely. Bitter. Unfulfilled. Excessive. A cautionary tale.

Not because she was any of those things — but because she needed to be. Narratives do not merely reflect culture. They discipline it.

If unmarried women could be imagined as content, marriage would lose its moral monopoly. So culture ensured they were not.

Throughout the 18th and 19th centuries, literature filled itself with tragic unmarried women: the lonely governess, the sharp-tongued aunt, the emotionally stunted schoolteacher. Rarely joyful. Rarely sexually fulfilled. Rarely powerful.

Stories taught reflexes. Readers absorbed the message without instruction: this is what happens if you do not attach.

Spinster panic was never about compassion. It was about containment. Contain women within marriage, and social order remains tidy. Allow women to flourish outside it, and expectations fracture.

Postwar Panic and the Return to the Home

The panic intensified whenever women demonstrated capacity without men.

After World War II, women had proven themselves economically indispensable. They worked. They earned. They ran households alone. They sustained nations.

And when the war ended, they were told to revert.

The cultural messaging was relentless: Fulfillment lives in the home. Happiness requires a husband. Independence is temporary. Marriage is destiny.

The unattached woman became symbolic — not merely of singleness, but of refusal. Refusal to retreat. Refusal to shrink. Refusal to return unpaid labour to the private sphere.

She was framed as unnatural. And unnatural things must be corrected.

Why Independent Women Destabilize Systems

Independent women do not destabilize society because they are chaotic. They destabilize it because they weaken leverage.

A woman who cannot survive alone is easier to control. A woman who fears social exile is easier to pressure. A woman who believes her value declines with age is easier to rush.

Remove these fears, and the entire negotiation changes.

An unattached woman negotiates from strength. She does not date for survival. She does not tolerate for security. She does not endure for legitimacy.

She evaluates. And evaluation is intolerable to systems built on urgency.

Historically, marriage functioned as an unequal bargain. Men gained lineage, labour, status, and sexual access. Women gained security.

But when women earn, own, inherit, and build independently, the bargain collapses.

Marriage becomes optional. And optional arrangements must justify themselves.

This is the quiet terror beneath the surface of cultural concern. "You're too picky.""You'll regret waiting." "Don't you want a family?"

These are not neutral questions. They are corrective signals. They mean: Return to the system.

Concern as Social Policing
Notice how rarely concern is directed upward.

A woman who tolerates emotional neglect is told relationships are hard. A woman who carries unequal labour is told compromise is necessary. A woman who stays despite exhaustion is praised for commitment.

But a woman who leaves — or declines entirely — is interrogated. Her motives are examined. Her psychology is questioned. Her femininity is doubted.

Concern is deployed not for her benefit, but for social equilibrium.

It is not her loneliness that worries people. It is her autonomy.

The Cultural Suspicion of Women Who Don't Center Men

A woman who does not center men is rarely allowed to exist neutrally.

If she prioritizes career, she is cold, or "a little bit too masculine". If she prioritizes friendships, she is avoiding intimacy. If she prioritises self-development, she is selfish. If she prioritises peace, she is bitter.

There must be something wrong.

Because femininity, as culturally constructed, is relational. To be feminine is to nurture, accommodate, harmonize, prioritize connection.

But connection has been narrowly defined: Connection to men.

When a woman redirects her emotional energy — toward herself, toward other women, toward creativity, toward rest — it is read as defiance. Not because it is loud. But because it reveals how much women's emotional labour has been propping up social life invisibly.

The Unpaid Emotional Infrastructure

Imagine removing women's unpaid emotional labour from society entirely.

Who generally smooths conflict in families? Who remembers birthdays, appointments, allergies, preferences? Who manages social continuity? Who absorbs male frustration at home? Who maintains relational memory?

Women do.

And an unattached woman — especially one at peace — opts out of automatic participation. She chooses where her energy goes. That choice exposes the assumption that her energy was always available.

And assumptions resent exposure.

The Economy of Female Availability

There is an economy built on female attachment. Dating apps. Engagement rings. Bridal industries. Weddings. Couples therapy. Anti-aging products marketed almost exclusively to women. Media narratives about "running out of time."

This is not conspiracy. It is commerce.

Fear is profitable.

A woman content alone does not rush. She does not panic-buy youth. She does not invest in romantic urgency. She becomes a poor consumer of anxiety. And when consumers disengage, industries escalate messaging.

Hence the resurgence of articles lamenting "lonely women." Hence the caricature of the "cat lady." Hence the moralising tone around women in their thirties.

Notice how rarely the same panic is applied to men. Male solitude does not destabilize the system in the same way — because men continue to benefit from women's emotional labour indirectly, even when unattached.

Women, by contrast, are told to secure one primary male relationship or risk social failure.

An unattached woman reallocates her investment. And reallocation is power.

The Fear of the Woman Who Leaves

There is another version of this threat: not the woman who never marries, but the woman who leaves.

A woman who exits a draining relationship calmly is profoundly unsettling. If she leaves angry, she can be dismissed as unstable. If she leaves devastated, she can be pitied.

But if she leaves and thrives? She becomes contagious.

Other women begin to imagine alternatives. They begin to re-evaluate endurance. They begin to question whether staying is virtue or habit.

This is why post-separation narratives emphasize regret. Loneliness. Hardship.

Not because those experiences never occur — but because their amplification discourages imitation.

The fear is not that women will be unhappy alone. It is that they might discover they are happier. And happiness spreads faster than anger.

The Quiet Confidence That Cannot Be Shamed

The most destabilising unattached woman is not militant. She is serene. She does not announce her independence. She does not argue online. She does not seek validation.

She simply lives differently. She invests in friendships. She builds financial autonomy. She rests. She travels. She dates selectively — or not at all.

And when warned that she might die alone, she does not flinch. Not because she knows the future. But because she is no longer afraid of the present.

Fear has long been the lever. Remove fear, and the lever snaps.

Reframing the "Threat"

The unattached woman is not a threat to society. She is a threat to systems built on female compliance.

She destabilizes the assumption that women will always prioritize relational harmony over personal clarity. She destabilizes the belief that male attention is the ultimate prize. She destabilizes the fiction that partnership is mandatory for fulfillment.

This is not destruction. It is evolution.

Every major social shift began with individuals declining inherited scripts. Women voting was once destabilising. Women working was once destabilising. Women owning property was once destabilising.

Women choosing peace over partnership may simply be the next shift.

The Truth Beneath the Warning

When people say, "You'll end up alone," they are not predicting your future. They are defending a structure.

They are articulating a fear that your refusal exposes something they were never allowed to consider. That completeness might be self-defined. That attachment might be optional. That peace might be preferable.

The unattached woman is inconvenient. She does not orbit. She does not apologize. She does not rush.

And in a world that has depended on women's fear to keep order, that calm is revolutionary.

She is not unfinished. She is ungoverned. And that is precisely why she is treated as a threat.

"You'll die alone."

Maybe. But I will not live incomplete.

And that is the part they find threatening.

Chapter 4

ROMANTIC PROPAGANDA

- Films, fiction, fairy tales.

- Why the grand gesture replaces emotional maturity.

- The addiction to intensity over stability.

Romance is not a private feeling.

It is a public ideology.

It did not emerge organically from human intimacy, nor does it exist merely to help people find connection. Romance, as women are taught to understand it, is a highly curated system of beliefs—repeated, aestheticized, rewarded, and defended across centuries of storytelling.

It is one of the most successful propaganda machines ever created.

Not because it lies outright. But because it distorts just enough to feel true.

Romantic propaganda does not need to persuade women that love exists. Women already know that. What it must persuade them of—what it has persuaded them of with astonishing efficiency—is that love looks a very specific way, unfolds along a very specific arc, and demands a very specific kind of female sacrifice.

Romantic propaganda teaches women that love is intense, destabilising, consuming. That it arrives suddenly. That it overwhelms reason. That it must be proven through endurance. That it is validated through suffering. That peace, by contrast, is suspicious. That stability is dull. That emotional maturity is passionless. That calm is something you "settle" for when you've failed to inspire desire.

These ideas are not incidental. They are structural. And they have consequences.

Because women do not merely consume romantic stories. They organize their lives around them.

Romance as Conditioning, Not Entertainment

We are encouraged to treat romance as harmless fantasy. Escapism. Pleasure. A guilty indulgence. Something women "just enjoy."

This framing is strategic. Because once something is classified as entertainment, it is exempt from critique. Once it is coded as fantasy, it is protected from accountability. Once it is labelled "what women like," it becomes unserious by default—despite the fact that it shapes women's expectations more powerfully than almost any formal education.

Romantic stories are not neutral. They are rehearsals. They teach women how to interpret attraction. How to measure worth. How to tolerate behaviour. How to override intuition. How to narrate dissatisfaction. How long to wait. How much to forgive. How to confuse anxiety with desire.

They do this long before women have language for consent, boundaries, or emotional health.

By the time a woman enters her first relationship, she is rarely inexperienced. She is simply trained.

Fairy Tales and the First Lie

Fairy tales are often dismissed as quaint cultural relics. Stories for children. Moral fables. Sweet nonsense. They are none of these.

Fairy tales are the first romantic instruction manuals most girls receive. And they follow a remarkably consistent structure.

The girl is incomplete. She is constrained. She suffers quietly. A man appears. Her suffering ends.

Rarely does the heroine solve her own problem. Rarely does she build power, competence, community, or autonomy. Rescue is external. Transformation is bestowed. Salvation arrives through selection.

The prince does not need to be evaluated. He does not need to demonstrate emotional capacity. He does not need to show consistency, care, or accountability. He merely arrives—desiring, decisive, chosen.

The message is absorbed long before it is conscious: Love happens *to* you. And it happens when you are chosen.

In these stories, love is instant. It requires no negotiation. No communication. No emotional labour. No repair. No boundaries. The relationship itself is the reward.

And the story ends before the work begins.

"Happily ever after" is not a conclusion. It is an erasure. It removes the woman from narrative complexity and deposits her into silence.

We never see her exhausted. We never see her managing moods. We never see her shrinking ambitions. We never see her negotiating unequal labour. We never see her giving in to sexual demands. We never see her loneliness inside the relationship.

The fairy tale ends precisely where women's real lives begin.

And that omission is not accidental.

The Evolution of the Hero—and the Consistency of His Deficits

As girls age, fairy tales evolve into novels, films, television, and prestige drama. The settings change. The costumes modernize. The language becomes more sophisticated.

But the romantic hero remains astonishingly consistent. He is distant but magnetic. He is brilliant but misunderstood. He is avoidant but intense. He is wounded. He is emotionally unavailable. He does not communicate clearly. He does not regulate his emotions. He does not offer consistency. He does not prioritize repair.

But he offers intensity. And intensity is framed as irresistible.

The woman's role is not to evaluate whether this man is capable of partnership. Her role is to endure until he changes.

Romantic narratives teach women that emotional dysfunction is not a warning sign—it is an invitation.

If she loves him enough, he will soften. If she waits long enough, he will open. If she sacrifices enough, she will be rewarded.

This is not intimacy. It is unpaid emotional labor disguised as destiny.

The Grand Gesture Scam

One of romantic propaganda's most effective sleights of hand is its replacement of emotional maturity with spectacle.

Men in romantic narratives are rarely required to be emotionally fluent. Instead, they are required to perform occasionally—and dramatically.

The grand gesture stands in for the daily work of emotional responsibility. He forgets her birthday—but plans a surprise trip. He ignores her needs—but declares his love publicly. He withdraws emotionally—but returns with intensity. He disappears—but comes back transformed for exactly one scene.

These gestures function as narrative resets. They wipe the slate clean without addressing the imbalance that made the gesture necessary in the first place.

They are emotional anaesthesia. They soothe conflict without resolving it. They interrupt accountability. They reward inconsistency. And because they are cinematic, they are deeply persuasive.

Women are trained to interpret these moments as proof of love rather than interruptions of neglect.

In real life, emotional maturity is unspectacular. It looks like reliability. It looks like follow-through. It looks like accountability without defensiveness. It looks like repair without theatrics. It looks like care without urgency.

These qualities do not photograph well. They do not score swelling music. They do not climax a plot. So they are excluded.

What replaces them is drama. And drama trains women to accept instability as romance.

Intensity: The Drug No One Names

Intensity is not romantic. It is neurochemical.

Uncertainty increases dopamine. Intermittent reward strengthens attachment. Emotional highs followed by emotional lows create bonding through relief.

This is not metaphor. It is biology.

Romantic narratives exploit this expertly. The on-again, off-again dynamic. The near-loss. The misunderstanding. The dramatic reconciliation.

These arcs keep audiences engaged—and women conditioned.

Stability does not activate the same neurological spikes. Calm does not feel urgent. Predictability does not feel intoxicating.

So calm is framed as boring. The woman who desires stability is told she is settling. The woman who chooses intensity is told she is passionate.

This framing is catastrophic. It trains women to override their nervous systems. It normalizes anxiety as attraction. It confuses longing with love. It teaches women to distrust peace.

Film, Fiction, and the Normalisation of Female Over-Functioning

Romantic films rarely depict functional relationships because functionality lacks conflict.

Instead, they rely on imbalance. The man is avoidant. The woman is adaptive. The plot depends on her emotional flexibility and his eventual revelation.

Notice how often the woman apologizes. Notice how often she waits. Notice how often she explains his behaviour to herself. Notice how often her boundaries dissolve for the sake of reunion.

And notice how rarely the man demonstrates sustained behavioural change. One confession. One kiss. One declaration.

Roll credits. The audience is satisfied.

The message lingers: love is proven through endurance.

The Aestheticisation of Female Suffering

In romantic fiction, women's suffering is made beautiful. The longing. The ache. The restraint. The dignified endurance of emotional deprivation.

Her pain is framed as depth. Her patience as virtue. Her silence as strength.

And when the relationship finally resolves—whether through union or tragedy—her suffering is retroactively justified.

This is deeply dangerous conditioning. It teaches women that pain becomes meaningful if it leads to connection. But pain that is only redeemed at the end is still pain endured unnecessarily. And real life does not guarantee happy endings.

Many women stay in draining relationships not because they are happy—but because they believe the suffering must mean something.

Romantic propaganda promises payoff. Reality often delivers repetition.

Why Emotional Immaturity Is Sexy on Screen

Emotionally immature men make excellent characters. They are unpredictable. They generate tension. They propel narrative.

Emotionally mature men resolve conflict quickly. They communicate clearly. They regulate themselves.

They are narratively inconvenient. So they are sidelined.

When they appear, they are often positioned as dull alternatives—the man the heroine must reject in order to pursue "real" passion.

This framing teaches women to associate emotional maturity with lack of chemistry.

And chemistry becomes synonymous with chaos.

This is not accidental.

It keeps women emotionally invested in unstable dynamics. And emotionally invested women are easier to exhaust.

The Gendered Burden of Repair

Romantic propaganda assigns repair work almost entirely to women. Women are expected to understand. To contextualize. To empathize. To wait.

"He had a hard childhood."

"He doesn't know how to express emotions."

"He's afraid of commitment."

These explanations are offered as reasons to stay—not warnings to leave.

Men's emotional limitations become women's responsibility to manage.

This is framed as intimacy. It is labour.

Romantic narratives rarely ask whether the man is capable of partnership. They ask whether the woman is patient enough.

The Pathologising of Female Peace

When women desire calm, romantic stories treat it as pathology. She is damaged. Closed off. Fearful. Avoidant. She must be persuaded back into chaos to be truly alive.

This framing delegitimizes women's desire for stability.

But many women do not desire peace because they fear love. They desire peace because they have experienced imbalance.

They are not closed. They are discerning.

Romantic propaganda refuses to acknowledge this—because acknowledging it would dismantle the fantasy.

What Believing the Story Costs

Women who internalize romantic propaganda struggle to leave unhealthy relationships. They interpret boredom as failure. Calm as absence. Stability as lack.

They chase intensity even as it destabilizes their lives.

And when they are exhausted, they blame themselves. "I'm too demanding." "I'm not patient enough." "I expect too much."

Rarely do they question the narrative itself.

Reclaiming Discernment

This chapter is not an argument against love. It is an argument against indoctrination.

Love does not require volatility. Connection does not require self-abandonment. Passion does not require instability.

These beliefs were taught. And they can be unlearned.

A woman who sees romantic propaganda begins to evaluate differently. She asks different questions. Does my body relax here? Is care consistent or episodic? Do words align with behaviour? Am I free—or simply managing? Is this connection nourishing—or consuming?

These questions disrupt the fantasy. And fantasy collapses under scrutiny.

Why Peace Feels Radical

When women step away from intensity-driven relationships, there is often withdrawal. Calm can feel unfamiliar. Silence can feel empty. Safety can feel flat.

This is not evidence that peace is wrong. It is evidence of conditioning.

The nervous system must relearn safety. The mind must relearn meaning.

Romantic propaganda trained women to equate stimulation with love. Undoing that association takes time. But on the other side of that discomfort is clarity.

The End of the Spell

Propaganda relies on repetition. Once named, it weakens. Once examined, it loses authority. Once questioned, it cannot command obedience.

A woman who sees the machinery of romance no longer mistakes chaos for chemistry.

She no longer confuses longing with love. She no longer waits for grand gestures to excuse daily neglect. She chooses differently.

Not because she fears being alone. But because she understands something she was never meant to understand:

Peace is not the absence of love. It is the absence of unnecessary suffering.

And that understanding changes everything.

Chapter 5

THE MALE FRAGILITY ECONOMY

- How some men depend on female emotional regulation.

- Why "needy" is often disguised as sensitive.

- The burden of constant reassurance.

Male fragility is not a personality trait. It is an economy.

It is a system that extracts emotional labor, attentiveness, reassurance, and self-silencing from women—and disguises that extraction as intimacy, sensitivity, or "being needed."

This economy does not operate on brute force. It operates on obligation. On guilt. On women's socialisation to soothe, anticipate, explain, soften, and stabilize the emotional lives of men who have never been required to do that work themselves.

It is one of the least examined power structures in modern heterosexual relationships, precisely because it does not look like power.

It looks like vulnerability.

Fragility as Currency

Male fragility is often framed as a deficit: men who are "bad at emotions," "not taught to communicate," "out of touch with their feelings."

This framing invites compassion—and compassion is quickly converted into responsibility.

Women are encouraged to see men's emotional limitations not as limitations, but as invitations. To help him open up. To teach him how to feel. To be patient while he learns. To make the environment safe enough for him to grow.

But notice what is missing from this story.

There is no parallel expectation that men learn to regulate themselves *before* entering relationships. There is no cultural insistence that men arrive emotionally literate, accountable, or self-soothing. Instead, women are positioned as the training ground.

Male fragility becomes a resource. Women become the infrastructure.

Emotional Regulation by Proxy

Many men do not regulate their emotions internally. They regulate them relationally.

They offload anxiety, insecurity, rage, uncertainty, and self-doubt onto the women closest to them—and then experience relief when those women absorb, soothe, and stabilize the emotional field.

This is not mutual regulation. It is delegation.

A woman becomes: The buffer between him and discomfort. The interpreter of his feelings. The manager of his self-esteem. The container for his volatility

When he is unsettled, she is expected to calm him. When he is insecure, she is expected to reassure him. When he is reactive, she is expected to de-escalate. When he withdraws, she is expected to pursue.

This labor is invisible because it is framed as love. But it is labor nonetheless. And it is relentless.

Why "Needy" Is Rebranded as "Sensitive"

Male neediness is rarely called what it is.

Instead, it is aestheticized. He is "emotionally deep." He is "in touch with his feelings." He is "not afraid to be vulnerable." He is "different from other men."

This reframing is powerful. It flatters both parties. The man is elevated above emotionally unavailable archetypes. The woman is positioned as special—chosen as the one he opens up to.

But scratch the surface, and the pattern is familiar.

His emotions are unprocessed. His insecurities are unmanaged. His self-worth is externally sourced. He requires constant reassurance—not because he is sensitive, but because he is unstable.

Sensitivity is the ability to perceive emotion. Fragility is the inability to hold it.

Romantic culture collapses the distinction.

The Reassurance Trap

One of the clearest markers of the male fragility economy is the demand for ongoing reassurance. Not occasional affirmation. Not mutual appreciation. But repetitive, compulsive emotional checking.

"Do you still love me?"
"Are you mad at me?"
"Are we okay?"
"Do you think I'm a good person?"

These questions are not neutral. They place the woman in a permanent evaluative role.

She becomes the mirror in which he confirms his worth.

And because reassurance provides temporary relief, the demand escalates. What worked last month no longer works this month. What worked yesterday doesn't work today.

The woman learns that her emotional availability must be constant—or the relationship destabilizes.

This creates a quiet tyranny. Her tone must be right. Her timing must be right. Her expressions must be carefully managed.

Because his emotional equilibrium depends on her responses.

This is not intimacy. It is dependency with better branding.

When His Feelings Outrank Reality

In the male fragility economy, men's feelings are treated as facts.

If he feels hurt, something must be wrong. If he feels threatened, someone must be at fault. If he feels insecure, the environment must change.

Often, that environment is the woman. She must soften her language. Lower her expectations. Limit her independence. Shrink her ambition. Reassure his relevance.

Any attempt to name this imbalance is met with defensiveness.

"You're attacking me."
"You're not being supportive."
"You're invalidating my feelings."

The conversation shifts instantly—from her experience to his emotional safety. And her original concern disappears.

The Cost to Women

Living inside the male fragility economy is exhausting.

Women become hyper-vigilant. They monitor mood shifts. They anticipate emotional fallout. They pre-empt conflict.

They learn to phrase truths gently. To delay needs. To carry anxiety that isn't theirs.

Over time, many women lose access to their own interiority. They are so busy managing his emotional climate that they forget to ask whether the relationship feels safe, reciprocal, or nourishing.

This is not accidental. A woman who is emotionally depleted is easier to contain. A woman who is busy regulating someone else is less likely to disrupt the system.

Why This Is Gendered

Men are not inherently fragile. They are *allowed* to be.

Boys are rarely required to develop emotional literacy. Men are rarely penalized for emotional incompetence.

Women are routinely expected to compensate.

This asymmetry is then romanticized.

"She understands him."
"She brings out his softer side."
"She's his anchor."

But anchoring someone who refuses to learn how to swim is not romance. It is unpaid labor with a love story attached.

The Illusion of Mutuality

The male fragility economy often masquerades as mutual emotional depth. Both partners talk about feelings. Both share vulnerabilities. Both value "openness."

But look closer.

Whose emotions dictate the pace of the relationship? Whose discomfort gets immediate attention? Whose needs require accommodation?

Mutuality is not about sharing feelings. It is about sharing responsibility.

When one person regulates and the other is regulated, the relationship is not equal—no matter how intimate it appears.

Why Women Stay

Many women stay in these dynamics because leaving feels cruel.

"He needs me."
"He'd fall apart without me."
"I'm the only one he opens up to."

This sense of indispensability is intoxicating—and entrapping. It converts care into obligation. And it ensures that the woman's departure feels like betrayal rather than self-preservation.

Reclaiming Emotional Sovereignty

A woman exits the male fragility economy when she stops managing emotions that are not hers. When she allows discomfort to exist. When she refuses to soothe insecurity she didn't create. When she declines responsibility for someone else's self-worth.

This does not make her cold. It makes her free.

The Quiet Revolution

Male fragility depends on women's compliance.

When women withdraw emotional over-functioning, the system destabilizes.

Some men adapt. Some grow. Some leave.

But the woman is no longer subsidising a dynamic that drains her life force.

And that, in itself, is radical.

Chapter 6

FEAR OF AGING AS A CONTROL MECHANISM

- The expiration myth.

- Why women are told desirability equals survival.

- Who profits from that fear.

The fear of aging was never about time.

It was about obedience.

From the moment a girl becomes aware of her body as visible, she is placed on a countdown she did not design. A countdown that tells her—quietly at first, then loudly—that her value is temporary, her relevance conditional, her desirability perishable.

This fear is not accidental. It is cultivated. Repeated. Monetized. And enforced.

A woman afraid of aging is a woman who rushes. A woman who rushes accepts less. A woman who accepts less is easier to control.

That is the function.

The Expiration Date Myth

Women are taught that they expire. Not metaphorically. Practically.

There is a supposed peak—usually vague, always young—and then a decline so steep it borders on social death. After this invisible line, women are told they become invisible, undesirable, unchosen, irrelevant.

The myth is remarkably consistent across cultures and eras, even as the "age" shifts conveniently to stay just ahead of women's lives.

First it is thirty. Then thirty-five. Then forty. Then "still attractive, but…"

The goalposts move, but the message does not.

Your value diminishes with time. Your options narrow. Your leverage weakens.

And crucially: **you are running out of time to secure a man.**

This is framed as concern. It is not. It is pressure.

Desirability as Survival

Women are not simply told that desirability is pleasant. They are told it is necessary.

Desirability is framed as:
- Economic safety

- Social legitimacy

- Emotional security

- Protection from loneliness

The implication is clear: if you are not chosen, you are at risk.

This turns romantic partnership from a preference into a survival strategy. And survival strategies override discernment.

A woman who believes she must secure partnership before time runs out is less likely to ask hard questions. Less likely to walk away. Less likely to demand reciprocity.

Fear compresses standards.

Why Men Are Not Given the Same Clock

Men age. Men change. Men get fat. Men wrinkle.

But men are rarely told they expire.

Instead, male aging is framed as:

- Maturity

- Authority

- Experience

- Depth

Older men are depicted as viable partners to younger women. Older women are depicted as cautionary tales.

This asymmetry is not biological. It is strategic.

A woman who believes men gain value with age while she loses it internalizes inferiority. She approaches relationships already negotiating from a deficit.

And a woman negotiating from a deficit is primed to overgive.

The Link Between Aging Fear and Male Fragility

Here is where the systems converge.

The male fragility economy requires women who:

- Over-function emotionally

- Tolerate inconsistency

- Accept reassurance roles

- Manage insecurity

But such labour is demanding. Sustaining it indefinitely would require women to believe they have limited alternatives.

Enter the expiration myth.

If a woman believes her desirability is fading, she is more likely to stay in draining dynamics. She is more likely to justify imbalance. More likely to tolerate neediness reframed as sensitivity.

Because leaving feels risky. What if she doesn't find someone else? What if this is her last chance? What if she's too old to start again?

Fear does the work that coercion no longer can.

The Panic Is Gendered for a Reason

Notice when the panic escalates.

Not when women are young and compliant. Not when they are busy proving worth.

But when women approach midlife. When experience accumulates. When illusions fall away. When tolerance decreases.

A woman with fewer illusions is dangerous to fragile systems. She has seen patterns. She recognizes emotional extraction. She is less impressed by grand gestures.

So the messaging intensifies.
"You don't want to end up alone."
"Dating only gets harder."
"Men don't want older women."

The aim is not accuracy. It is urgency.

Who Profits from the Fear

Follow the money.

The beauty industry profits from women believing aging is failure. The cosmetic industry profits from women fearing visibility loss. The dating industry profits from romantic urgency. The wedding industry profits from rushed decisions.

But so do relational dynamics built on female accommodation.

A woman afraid of aging is easier to rush into commitment. Easier to guilt into patience. Easier to silence with scarcity logic. Fear keeps her investing—even when returns diminish.

The Myth of the "Lonely Older Woman"
One of the most persistent threats used to discipline women is the image of the lonely older woman.

She is portrayed as bitter, regretful, isolated, surrounded by reminders of what she failed to secure

This image is not representative. It is disciplinary. It exists to warn younger women what happens when they do not comply.

But here is what is rarely shown: Older women often report:
- Greater peace

- Stronger friendships

- Increased self-trust

- Less tolerance for nonsense

Loneliness is not exclusive to singleness. Nor is companionship guaranteed by partnership. But the myth persists because it is useful.

Why Women Are Told They'll "End Up" Alone
Notice the language.

Men are rarely described as "ending up" alone.

Women are. As if solitude is a punishment. As if it is the result of failure.

As if it is not sometimes a choice.

This framing strips women of agency and recasts autonomy as loss.

It implies that partnership is the default destination—and anything else is a deviation.

But destinations are not defaults. They are decisions.

Aging as Liberation (The Unspoken Truth)

What threatens systems most is not young women.

It is older women who are no longer afraid. Women who have:

- Decentered male approval

- Outgrown emotional labour roles

- Recognized extraction patterns

- Reclaimed time and energy

These women are not desperate. They are **selective**.

And selectivity is intolerable to systems that rely on female overavailability.

So their narratives are suppressed.

The Reversal No One Mentions

There is a quiet reversal that occurs when women age without surrendering themselves to fear.

They gain leverage.

Not sexual leverage defined narrowly—but existential leverage.

They are less persuadable by intensity. Less impressed by performative vulnerability. Less willing to manage fragility.

They choose peace not as consolation—but as preference.

And that preference is radical.

Aging Fear as Behavioural Control

Fear of aging does not just affect how women feel. It affects how they behave. It encourages:

- Staying longer than staying healthy

- Accepting ambiguity instead of clarity

- Over-functioning to remain "valuable"

- Prioritising being chosen over choosing

It narrows possibility. And narrow possibility keeps women compliant.

Rewriting the Timeline

What if aging were not framed as loss—but as accumulation?

Accumulation of:

- Pattern recognition

- Emotional literacy

- Boundary clarity

- Nervous system wisdom

What if time increased discernment rather than erased worth?

This reframing collapses urgency. And without urgency, manipulation struggles to survive.

Peace Is Not a Consolation Prize

Women are often told that peace is what they choose when passion fails.

This is a lie. Peace is what women choose when they refuse unnecessary suffering.

Peace is not passive.It is not resignation. It is not fear-based.

It is an informed choice.

The Final Threat

The greatest threat is not the woman who ages.

It is the woman who ages **without panic**.
She does not rush.
She does not settle.
She does not negotiate against herself.
She understands that partnership is optional—not mandatory.

And optionality dissolves control.

The Fear Loses Its Power

Once a woman stops believing that aging diminishes her worth, the system loses its leverage.

She no longer accepts fragility as intimacy. She no longer trades peace for reassurance. She no longer fears solitude more than imbalance.

She is not immune to loneliness. But she is immune to manipulation.

And that immunity is the quiet revolution running underneath everything.

PART II: THE COST

What Women Give Away in Order to Stay

B y now the machinery is visible.

You have seen the stories. The scripts. The promises that taught women to fear their own independence.

You have seen how romance was polished into myth. How solitude was framed as failure. How the quiet threat—*You will die alone*—was deployed like a cultural weapon.

Part I exposed the lie.

But lies are never harmless. They are investments. And investments are made for a reason.

Because somewhere, someone profits when women believe that partnership is the price of safety. Or legitimacy. Or worth.

This section is not about theory.

It is about cost. Not the dramatic costs that make headlines—divorce courts, scandals, public betrayals. The quieter ones.

The costs that accumulate slowly enough to be mistaken for normal life.

Ambition softened so a man does not feel small.

Opinions edited so a dinner table stays calm.

Energy redirected into managing moods that were never yours to manage.

Desire negotiated. Silence practiced. Time surrendered.

Year by year, the ledger grows.

Women are taught to call this compromise. To call it maturity. To call it love.

But if you examine the pattern closely, something else emerges.

A transfer. Of labor. Of attention. Of emotional stability. From women... to men.

This is the quiet economy beneath the romantic story. And like any economy, it runs on extraction.

Part II is not an accusation.

It is an inventory. A careful accounting of the subtle ways women are asked—often lovingly, often invisibly—to make themselves smaller in order to maintain the structure around them.

Some readers will recognize these patterns immediately.

Others may feel a flicker of discomfort. That discomfort is not a problem. It is recognition beginning.

Because once a woman begins to see the cost clearly, something changes.

The question is no longer: *How do I make this work?*

The question becomes: *Why am I paying for it at all?*

Chapter 7

Emotional Labor: The Invisible Tax

- Therapy without the credentials.

- Managing moods, smoothing egos, translating feelings.

- Why women are exhausted.

There is a tax on women that does not appear on any payslip.

It is not deducted by the government. It is deducted by men.

It is paid in sighs swallowed. In words softened. In tempers pre-empted. In moods managed. In the constant, grinding vigilance of keeping the emotional weather stable so that a grown man does not storm.

This is emotional labor. And women have been paying it for centuries. Unpaid. Unacknowledged. Expected.

You are told partnership means sharing. But what you are often handed is management. You are not his lover, you are his regulator. You are not his equal, you are his emotional mother.

And your nervous system has been paying the interest.

Therapy Without the Credentials

He says he doesn't believe in therapy. But he believes in you.

He doesn't journal. He doesn't read about attachment styles. He doesn't examine his childhood. He doesn't interrogate his temper. He doesn't unpack his shame.

He comes home and hands it to you instead.

And you, because you are loving and capable and well-trained, take it.

You translate his silence. You interpret his withdrawal. You decode his irritability. You ask the right questions in the right tone at the right time.

You know when he's "not really angry" but stressed. You know when he's "not really cold" but scared. You know when he's "not really critical" but insecure.

You have become a forensic emotional investigator. You do this without a degree. Without supervision. Without rest.

You listen to stories about his boss. You soothe wounds inflicted by his father. You reassure him that he is enough. You absorb his anxiety about money, status, performance.

And then you ask him about his day. He says, "Fine."

You say, "Just fine?"

Because you know. You always know.

He calls you his rock.

Of course he does. Rocks don't require soothing. Rocks don't crack under pressure. Rocks absorb impact.

He loves that you are sturdy. But rocks erode.

Managing Moods Like It's a Second Job

Women do not merely experience their own emotions. We anticipate his. We track them. We modify our behavior accordingly.

Is he tired? Better not bring up the thing that upset you.

Is he stressed? Better make dinner lighter, conversation softer.

Is he quiet? Better ask gently if something's wrong.

Is he loud? Better de-escalate before it becomes a fight.

You become a climate scientist in a house where the forecast depends on his mood. You learn to read micro-expressions. The tightening jaw. The shallow breath. The clipped answer.

You pivot. You smooth. You adjust.

And if the evening goes well, he says, "See? We never fight."

No, you don't. Because you do the labor before the explosion. You are the sandbag wall around his emotional river.

And he mistakes your prevention for harmony.

Smoothing Egos

Men are not encouraged to sit with discomfort. They are encouraged to defend against it.

So when a man feels small, he may become sharp. When he feels incompetent, he may become critical. When he feels insecure, he may become controlling.

And you, because you are perceptive, recognize it. You see the boy beneath the bluster. You soften.

You praise him for things he did adequately. You reassure him about things that were never in question. You downplay your own success so he does not feel diminished. You laugh at jokes that were not funny. You shrink your brilliance so he can feel large.

You call it kindness and understanding. It is labor. You tell yourself it is compassionate to understand his fragility. But who is holding yours?

When you feel small, do you get to lash out? When you feel insecure, do you get to control? When you feel incompetent, do you get to withdraw and have someone gently decode you? Or are you expected to regulate yourself before you even speak?

Women are raised to self-monitor. Men are raised to be accommodated.

This is not romance. It is asymmetry.

Translating Feelings He Won't Name

You say, "What are you feeling?"

He says, "Nothing."

You say, "You seem off."

He says, "I'm fine."

But he isn't. He is overwhelmed. Or ashamed. Or resentful. Or frightened.

But he does not have the language. Or the practice. Or the willingness. Or the emotional intelligence.

So you become translator. You suggest options. "Are you stressed about work?" "Are you worried about money?" "Did something I say upset you?"

You offer emotional vocabulary like flashcards. You gently guide him toward recognition. You coax. You wait.

And sometimes, after 45 minutes of delicate excavation, he says, "Yeah... maybe I'm just stressed."

And he feels relieved. He thinks he figured it out.

You did. You excavated it from him like an archaeologist brushing dust from an artifact.

And you are tired. Because this was not one conversation. It was the hundredth.

Why Women Are Exhausted

You are not exhausted because you are weak. You are exhausted because you are carrying two nervous systems. Yours. And his.

You monitor the relational atmosphere. You remember birthdays. You manage social calendars. You initiate difficult conversations. You check in about the emotional temperature of the relationship.

You hold the invisible thread that keeps the connection intact.

If you drop it, it frays.

He says, "Why didn't you tell me it was bothering you?"

Because you were busy managing you.

He says, "I didn't know you needed help."

Because you are so competent he assumes you require none.

He says, "You should have asked."

You did. Gently. Indirectly. Three times.

You think, " I shouldn't have to ask."

But you are so used to cushioning requests that he does not hear urgency.

So you get louder.

And then he says you are overreacting. And you begin to wonder if maybe you are.

You are not. You are depleted. There is a difference.

The Good Girlfriend Trap

You have been trained to be "low maintenance."

To not be "too much." To not nag. Not push. Not demand.

You pride yourself on being understanding. You are the cool one. The reasonable one. The one who doesn't start drama.

You absorb. You adjust. You forgive.

Until one day you are furious about something small. The dishes. The tone. The forgotten plan.

And he is bewildered. "Where is this coming from?"

It is coming from years of emotional invoices you never sent.

You thought love meant generosity without ledger. But generosity without boundaries becomes self-abandonment.

You were not low maintenance. You were high tolerance. And tolerance without reciprocity becomes resentment.

Emotional Labor Is Gendered

Yes, men experience emotions. Yes, men suffer.

But who is expected to manage the relationship?

When a relationship falters, who is told to communicate better? Who buys the books? Who listens to the podcasts? Who suggests couples counseling? Who schedules it? Who says, "We need to talk"?

Rarely the man who benefits from the current arrangement.

When he does seek therapy, it is often because she insisted. When he learns emotional language, it is often because she modeled it.

And if she leaves?

Suddenly he is "blindsided." He did not see it coming because he was not tracking the emotional undercurrent.

She was. She always was.

The Mothering of Men

There is a quiet shift that happens in many relationships.

At first you are lovers. Then you become guide. Then manager. Then mother.

You remind him of appointments. You encourage him to call his family. You help him draft difficult emails. You tell him where to put the apostrophes. You advise him on conflict. You help him process friendships.

He leans on you. And leaning becomes dependence. And dependence becomes entitlement.

He expects you to be calm when he is chaotic. Stable when he is volatile. Empathetic when he is dismissive.

He says he loves how nurturing you are. Of course he does – it saves him from growing up.

And you begin to feel something you cannot name. It is not quite anger. It is not quite sadness.

It is the slow erosion of eroticism. Because it is very hard to desire someone you are raising.

The Emotional Double Standard

When a woman is upset, she is emotional. When a man is upset, he is stressed.

When a woman raises her voice, she is hysterical. When a man raises his voice, he is passionate.

When a woman cries, she is manipulative. When a man withdraws, he is processing.

The standard is crooked. Women are expected to be both expressive and composed. To articulate feelings beautifully without burdening anyone. To be vulnerable without being overwhelming. To be strong without being cold.

And if she fails? She is difficult.

So she learns to calibrate. To pre-filter. To edit.

He does not. He simply feels. And expects accommodation.

The Cost to Your Body

Chronic emotional labor does not stay in the mind.

It settles in the body. In the jaw that clenches. In the stomach that tightens. In the shoulders that rise unconsciously. In the fatigue that sleep does not fix.

You think you are tired from work. But you are tired from vigilance. You are tired from pre-empting conflict. You are tired from anticipating reaction. You are tired from being the emotional shock absorber.

Peace is not the absence of noise. Peace is the absence of bracing. And many women have never known that in partnership.

"But He's a Good Man"
Of course he is.

Most men are not villains. They are simply unpracticed. Unexamined. Unaccustomed to being required to carry emotional weight.

He may love you deeply. He may never intend harm. But intention does not erase impact.

If you are his primary source of emotional regulation, that is weight. If you are his only safe place to unravel, that is weight. If you are expected to be steady while he fluctuates freely, that is weight.

Love does not mean you must carry disproportionate load.

Good men can still benefit from unequal labor. Kind men can still lean too hard. Decent men can still exhaust you.

Why You Didn't Notice
Because it was gradual. Because you are capable. Because you believed love meant generosity. Because he praised your empathy. Because you are strong. Because you are proud of being strong. And because women are socialized to equate self-sacrifice with virtue.

You did not notice the imbalance because it did not arrive as cruelty. It arrived as need.

And you are compassionate.

What Equal Emotional Labor Looks Like

It looks like a man who can name his feelings without being coached. It looks like a man who initiates repair. It looks like a man who says, "I was defensive. That's on me." It looks like a man who manages his stress without making it your problem. It looks like a man who notices your exhaustion before you collapse.

It looks like shared responsibility for the relational climate. It looks like you not being the only one who says, "We need to talk." It looks like you not being the only adult in the room.

The Radical Act of Dropping the Rope

What happens if you stop translating? If you stop smoothing? If you stop anticipating?

At first, chaos.nHe may bristle. He may accuse you of being distant. He may say you have changed.

You have.

You have stopped subsidizing his emotional development. You have stopped paying the invisible tax. And suddenly he feels the cost.

That discomfort? That is growth trying to happen. Or it is exposure.

Either way, it is no longer yours to manage.

Peace Is Not Coldness

When women choose peace over partnership, they are accused of being bitter. Of giving up. Of being too independent.

But peace is not isolation. Peace is the absence of unpaid labor. Peace is not having to anticipate someone else's emotional volatility. Peace is not editing yourself to protect a fragile ego. Peace is not translating feelings for someone who refuses to learn the language. Peace is coming home and not bracing.

And once you experience that, you understand something radical: Partnership is not automatically better than solitude.

Only equal partnership is.

Anything else is employment.

The Final Question

If you removed the emotional management from your relationship—the reminders, the soothing, the decoding, the smoothing, the anticipating—what would remain?

A partner? Or a boy waiting to be regulated?

You are not required to be anyone's therapist Not without credentials. Not without pay. Not without reciprocity.

You are allowed to want a man who can hold his own weight. You are allowed to rest. You are allowed to stop being the emotional infrastructure.

Because the invisible tax has been levied on women long enough.

And peace, dear reader, is wealth.

The Ledger

Partnership, women are told, is supposed to expand your life. But for many women, it quietly becomes a system of containment.

Not dramatic enough to be called abuse. Not equal enough to be called partnership. Just exhausting enough to slowly hollow you out.

And that is where this book must now go.

Because once the lie is understood, a harder question appears:

Not why women stay. But what staying actually *costs* them.

That is where we are going next.

Chapter 8

Shrinking to Be Loved

- Dimmed ambition.

- Softened opinions.

- Self-editing to avoid male insecurity.

There is a particular kind of violence that leaves no bruises. It is not loud. It is not dramatic. It does not announce itself as oppression.

It is quiet.

It is the moment you lower your voice mid-sentence. The moment you laugh and say, "Oh, it's not a big deal." The moment you describe your promotion as "just a little thing." The moment you pretend you don't care that you were overlooked.

It is the art of becoming smaller.

So he can stay comfortable. So he can stay big. So he can stay.

Women are not only taught to be desirable. We are taught to be digestible.

And brilliance is hard to digest.

The First Time You Learned
You did not wake up one day and decide to dim yourself.

You were trained. Maybe it was in school. You got the results. You answered too many questions. You won the prize.

And the boys rolled their eyes. "Know-it-all." "Goody-two-shoes."

You learned something that day: Intelligence must be portioned carefully.

Maybe it was in your first relationship. You spoke passionately about politics, art, religion, money.

He teased you. "Why are you so intense?"

You laughed. You softened. You said, "Sorry, I get carried away."

Carried away by what? Your own mind?

Maybe it was subtler.

You got the job he wanted. You earned more. You were more qualified.

He did not say anything cruel. He simply withdrew. A slight chill. A quiet distance.

And you felt it. So you recalibrated. Not because he demanded it. Because you wanted connection.

And women will amputate pieces of themselves before they will risk abandonment.

Dimmed Ambition

Ambition in men is attractive. It is drive. It is hunger. It is leadership.

Ambition in women is threatening. It may be considered selfish, intimidating and emasculating.

So women learn to disguise it.

You say you're "just exploring options." You say you're "not sure what's next." You downplay the five-year plan in your head. You pretend you're flexible when you are focused. You minimize your hunger so he does not feel small next to it.

If you are more successful, you are told to reassure him. If you are more driven, you are told to soften. If you are more disciplined, you are told not to "pressure" him.

And slowly, ambition becomes something you experience privately. You achieve quietly. You negotiate gently. You celebrate modestly. You become extraordinary in ways that do not disrupt his self-image.

And this is called love. In reality, it is distortion.

The Economics of Female Success

In heterosexual relationships, there is an unspoken economy. If he earns more, it is natural. If she earns more, it is complicated.

If he works long hours, he is committed. If she works long hours, she is neglectful.

If he prioritizes career, she supports him. If she prioritizes career, he questions compatibility.

You begin to measure your growth against his comfort. Should I apply for the promotion? Should I relocate? Should I outpace him? You are told to consider the relationship.

But who is told to consider you?

The number of brilliant women who have turned down opportunity to preserve a man's ego could fund entire nations.

You told yourself it was compromise. But compromise implies mutual adjustment.

Shrinking is not compromise. It is concession.

Softened Opinions

You have strong opinions. On politics. On money. On parenting. On ethics. On how the world should work.

But you have learned that strong female opinions are "aggressive."

So you preface. "This might be silly, but…" "I could be wrong…" "Don't get mad, but…"

You cushion your truth before you speak it. You present it like fragile glass. You watch his face for reaction.

If he bristles, you retreat. If he debates, you soothe. If he mocks, you laugh.

You become adept at rhetorical gymnastics. Not to win. To avoid conflict.

And he calls you easygoing.

You are not easygoing. You are strategic.

Self-Editing as Survival

Self-editing is exhausting.

You scan your thoughts before you release them:
Is this too much?
Too sharp?
Too feminist?
Too critical?
Too ambitious?
Too emotional?
Too intelligent?

You trim. You tailor. You moderate.

You say 70% of what you think. You express 50% of what you feel. You reveal 30% of what you desire.

Because you have learned that full-volume womanhood is destabilizing.

You have watched men withdraw from women who challenge them. You have seen them label such women "difficult."

You have internalized the warning. So you become palatable. And palatable women are praised.

The Fear Beneath It

Let us be honest. This is not just about ego. It is about fear.

You fear being alone. You fear that if you are fully yourself, no one will stay.

Because you have been told, explicitly and implicitly, that men prefer softness to sharpness.

They say they want strong women. But often they mean resilient, not formidable.

They want a woman who can endure. Not a woman who can outshine.

So you negotiate with your own magnitude.

How much of me can I show without being abandoned?
How much brilliance can I reveal without destabilizing him?

And every time you choose less, something inside you registers it. Even if you cannot name it.

The Subtle Sabotage

Sometimes he does not ask you to shrink. He simply resists your expansion.

You start a new project. He jokes about it.

You go back to study. He questions the cost.

You speak passionately. He rolls his eyes, saying you're too emotive.

You out-earn him. He may withdraw sexually.

Nothing overt. Nothing dramatic. Just small discouragements. Death by a thousand diminutions.

You begin to associate growth with friction. So you slow down.

Not because you lack drive but because you crave peace. And shrinking feels like the easier route.

Until one day you look in the mirror and do not recognize the woman staring back.

The Cost to Desire

Here is the irony. Men are often drawn to your fire in the beginning. Your intelligence. Your ambition. Your sharpness.

It excites them. It challenges them. It makes you different.

But if they do not grow alongside you, that same fire begins to threaten.

So you reduce the flame. And something strange happens.

He becomes comfortable. And you become bored.

Because you cannot respect someone who requires your diminishment to feel secure. And you cannot desire someone you must protect from yourself.

Sex becomes mechanical. Conversations become shallow. You feel restless.

He says, "You've changed."

You have.

You are suffocating.

Women Who Outgrow Their Relationships

Growth is not neutral. When one partner evolves and the other resists, tension forms.

Women are often the ones evolving. Reading. Reflecting. Healing. Expanding.

If he remains static, your growth exposes the gap. You begin to see patterns you once tolerated. You begin to articulate needs you once swallowed. You begin to want more. And he may interpret that as dissatisfaction.

It is. But not because you are greedy. Because you are awake.

You can either shrink back into compatibility. Or continue growing and risk the fracture.

Many women choose fracture. Not because they hate men. Because they refuse to amputate themselves any longer.

The Myth of "Intimidating" Women

A woman is called intimidating when she refuses to shrink. When she speaks clearly. When she earns well. When she expects competence. When she does not fawn.

Intimidating is often code for: "I cannot dominate you." Or: "I do not feel automatically superior to you."

Men who are secure are not threatened by capable women. They are energized by them.

But insecurity is common. And instead of confronting it, some men prefer women who stay smaller.

So you must decide. Do you want to be comforting? Or fully expressed?

Because sometimes, tragically, you cannot be both with the same man.

The Internal Split

Shrinking creates a fracture within.

Outwardly, you are agreeable. Inwardly, you are roaring.

Outwardly, you are supportive. Inwardly, you are resentful.

Outwardly, you are "easy." Inwardly, you are suffocating.

This split manifests as anxiety. As irritability. As unexplained sadness.

You tell yourself you should be grateful. He is kind. He is stable. He is decent.

But you feel smaller. And the body knows when it is compressed.

The Praise for Smallness

Society rewards women who do not threaten male dominance. You are called nurturing. Graceful. Elegant. Understanding.

You are admired for making space. Rarely are you admired for taking it.

When you assert, you are abrasive. When you negotiate hard, you are difficult. When you expect excellence, you are demanding.

So you calibrate. You become masterful at occupying just enough space to function, but not enough to disrupt.

And you tell yourself this is maturity. But maturity is not self-erasure. It is integration.

Love That Requires Diminishment Is Not Love

Let us say it plainly. If a man can only love you at 70% of your capacity, he does not love you. He loves the edited version.

If your success threatens him, he is not your partner. He is your ceiling.

If your opinions destabilize him, he is not your equal. He is your project.

And you are not obligated to shrink for someone who refuses to expand.

Love is not a cage built from compliments. It is not "I love how you're not like other women." It is not "You're strong, but not intimidating." It is not conditional admiration.

Real love expands you. It does not require contraction.

The Loneliness Lie Revisited

You are told that if you do not soften, you will be alone. That men do not like strong women. That you must choose between power and partnership.

This is the loneliness lie.

The lie says: **Better smaller and loved than full and alone.**

But alone at full capacity is not emptiness. It is freedom.

And partnership at half-capacity is not love. It is containment.

Which is lonelier?

A quiet house where you can stretch? Or a shared bed where you must fold yourself nightly?

The Radical Refusal

There comes a moment. A small one. When you say the full sentence. When you apply for the promotion. When you speak your unfiltered opinion. When you stop apologizing for ambition. When you refuse to downplay success.

It feels terrifying. It feels like risk. Because it is.

Some men will leave, but only if they have someone to leave for.

Some will bristle. Some will attempt to reassert dominance.

And some will rise.

The ones who rise are rare. But they exist. And they are worth waiting for.

What Expansion Feels Like

Expansion feels like exhaling fully. It feels like laughing loudly without scanning the room. It feels like stating what you want without cushioning. It feels like celebrating yourself without embarrassment. It feels like ambition without apology. It feels like taking up space.

And if a man cannot breathe in that atmosphere, he was never meant to inhabit it.

You Were Never Too Much

You were only too much for someone committed to being less.

Your ambition was not the problem. His stagnation was.

Your intelligence was not abrasive. His insecurity was.

Your clarity was not aggressive. His fragility was.

We women must stop internalizing the discomfort of those who benefit from our diminishment.

Final Reckoning

Look at your life.

Where have you softened unnecessarily? Where have you edited? Where have you chosen harmony over honesty? Where have you reduced your hunger?

Now ask:

What would happen if I stopped? Not gradually. Not apologetically.

But decisively.

What would grow in the space where shrinking once lived? What opportunities would open? What kind of partner would remain?

Because here is the truth they do not print in bridal magazines: The right man is not threatened by your expansion. He is relieved by it. He does not need you smaller. He needs you real.

And if being real costs you certain men, then let it.

You were not built to be palatable. You were built to be powerful.

And power, dear reader, does not whisper.

It stands. Full height. Unapologetic. Unshrunk.

Chapter 9

The Anxiety of Managing a Grown Man

- Weaponized incompetence.

- Passive dependence.

- The "I just need you" trap.

There is a specific kind of anxiety that women in unequal relationships carry. It is not dramatic. It does not present as crisis. It hums.

It is the low-level vigilance of knowing that if you do not manage the situation, something will unravel. A bill will go unpaid. A conflict will escalate. A social obligation will be forgotten. A responsibility will slide quietly into your lap.

You are not partnered. You are supervising. And supervision requires alertness.

This is the anxiety of managing a grown man.

Weaponized Incompetence

Let us begin plainly. Weaponized incompetence is not about intelligence. It is about avoidance.

It looks like this: "I'm just not good at that." "You do it better." "I didn't know." "You should've told me."

He burns dinner. He shrinks laundry. He forgets the appointment. He "messes up" the school form. He loads the dishwasher like an abstract sculpture.

You correct him. He sighs. Eventually, you do it yourself. Peace restored. Efficiency regained.

He has learned something. If he performs incompetence convincingly enough, you will assume responsibility. And you will tell yourself he's trying.

This pattern is ancient. Men are not incompetent. They are unrequired.

Call-Out: **THIS IS CONDITIONING.**

When a man consistently fails at tasks he performs competently at work, with friends, or in hobbies, it is not inability. It is selective disengagement.

He can manage spreadsheets, machinery, code, contracts.

But he cannot remember the pediatrician's name. He cannot figure out how to buy the correct brand of detergent. He cannot anticipate what needs doing.

And so you anticipate. Because someone must.

He says, "Just tell me." You think, "I shouldn't *have* to".

The Mental Load

The visible tasks are exhausting. The invisible tracking is worse.

You remember: Birthdays. Medication refills. Holiday logistics. Family tensions. Household supplies. Repair schedules. Emotional undercurrents.

You are the relational project manager.

He may "help." But help implies the project belongs to you.

You are the default. He is the assistant.

And assistants do not wake up at 2 a.m. mentally cataloguing what has not yet been done. You do.

The anxiety is not from the tasks. It is from the knowledge that if you release control, things degrade.

And you do not want degradation. You want stability. So you grip tighter.

Passive Dependence

Some men do not demand. They lean.

They do not dominate. They defer.

They look to you for decisions. "Whatever you want." "You're better at that." "I trust you."

It sounds flattering. It feels suffocating.

Because what is framed as trust is often abdication. He does not choose the restaurant. He does not choose the holiday. He does not choose the sofa. He does not choose conflict resolution.

He waits. And waiting transfers weight. Soon you are choosing everything.

If it goes well, you both enjoy it. If it goes badly, it's your fault. You feel responsible.

He shrugs. You spiral. This is the quiet tyranny of passivity.

The "I Just Need You" Trap

Need can be intoxicating.

To be needed is to feel important. Indispensable. Chosen.

He says: "I don't know what I'd do without you." "You keep me together." "You're my rock."

It sounds like devotion. But it is dependence. And dependence, when unequal, breeds anxiety.

Because if you are his regulator, if you are his planner, if you are his emotional stabilizer, you cannot collapse, nor falter, nor rest.

If you are the structure, who holds you?

You begin to monitor your own exhaustion carefully. Because if you break, the system fails. And the system is him.

The Performance of Helplessness

Watch closely.

He navigates airports alone. He negotiates salary. He argues politics confidently.

But at home, he is confused.

The washing machine is mysterious. The birthday gift selection is overwhelming. The childcare routine is complicated.

Helplessness appears precisely where responsibility would cost him comfort.

You begin to resent it.

Then you feel guilty for resenting it. Because he's "not malicious." Intent is irrelevant to impact. You are anxious because you cannot rely on him.

And reliance is the foundation of adult partnership.

Without it, you are not two adults. You are caretaker and he is dependent.

Hyper-Competence as Coping

Women in these dynamics often become hyper-competent.

You anticipate before asked. You research before needed. You solve before crisis. You pride yourself on handling everything.

But hyper-competence is often trauma response.

You learned early that stability depended on you. So you create it.

You manage not because you love control. You manage because chaos is costly.

But management becomes identity. If you stop, who are you? And what falls apart?

The anxiety is not simply about him. It's about the collapse of a system you have built around his avoidance.

The Slow Build of Irritation

At first, it is minor.

You remind him to call the plumber. You resend the email he forgot. You double-check the booking he was supposed to confirm.

You laugh about it.

Over time, the laughter thins. You begin to notice the asymmetry.

You are vigilant. He is relaxed. You are tracking. He is drifting.

You begin to feel something sharp. Not rage. Irritation.

Irritation is anger's quieter sibling. It accumulates.

And because you are managing so much, you have no space to process it. So it seeps out sideways. A snapped comment. A cold tone.

He asks, "Why are you so stressed?"

Because I am carrying us.

Anxiety as Baseline

Your nervous system adapts to constant oversight.

You are always half-alert. Even in rest, you are scanning.

Did he pay that? Did he book that? Did he follow through?

You check. He forgets. You fix.

Your body registers unpredictability. And unpredictability breeds anxiety.

Even if he is kind. Even if he is loving. If he is unreliable, you are never fully at ease.

Peace requires trust. Trust requires competence. Competence requires ownership. Ownership is what he has quietly avoided.

When You Become His Mother

This is the shift no one warns you about.

You start reminding. You start correcting. You start instructing.

He resists. You push. He withdraws. You escalate.

The dynamic calcifies. You sound like a parent. He behaves like a teenager.

Desire evaporates. Respect erodes.

You do not want to mother him. He does not want to be mothered.

But the system you both participate in creates exactly that.

And anxiety becomes chronic. Because you cannot relax around a child. And you cannot desire someone you supervise.

Case Study: Laura

Laura was 38 when she left.

Her husband was not cruel. He was charming, creative, "laid back."

He forgot bills. He missed deadlines. He started projects and abandoned them.

Laura picked up the slack. She managed finances. She scheduled everything. She soothed his work frustrations. She reminded him to call his mother.

He called her controlling. She felt exhausted.

When she left, the first thing she noticed was not sadness. It was silence in her body.

She stopped checking her phone for mistakes he might have made. She stopped anticipating.

She slept. Her loneliness was clean. Her anxiety disappeared.

The Gendered Expectation

If a woman behaves incompetently, she is shamed.

If a man behaves incompetently at home, he is teased. "Typical man." "Men are useless."

The joke protects the pattern.

Incompetence becomes personality. And personality becomes excuse.

But incompetence is rarely universal. It is selective. And selective incompetence benefits one party.

Why You Stay

You tell yourself: He's good in other ways. He tries. He didn't have good role models. He'll grow.

Maybe he will. But growth requires discomfort.

And if you cushion every consequence, he never feels it. You prevent disaster. So he never learns prevention.

Your competence enables his stagnation.

And that knowledge is uncomfortable. Because it means your love participates in your anxiety.

The Invisible Contract

Unspoken but present: You will handle the details. You will manage the emotions. You will stabilize the system.

In return, he will… what? Love you? Provide financially? Be loyal?

If the exchange is unequal, anxiety follows.

Because you know the contract is lopsided.

You feel it. Even if you never articulate it. And once you see it, you cannot unsee it.

The Breaking Point

The breaking point rarely arrives with drama.

It arrives with fatigue.

One more forgotten thing. One more emotional meltdown. One more moment of realizing you are alone in responsibility.

You do not explode. You withdraw.

Something in you shuts down.

He senses distance. He panics. He promises change.

You have heard promises before.

What you crave is not words. It is relief. Relief from management. Relief from supervision. Relief from being the only adult in the room.

The Radical Question

What would happen if you stopped managing? If you let the bill go unpaid? If you let the appointment be missed? If you refused to rescue?

Fear rises.

Because you are not just protecting him. You are protecting your own stability.

But until consequences land where they belong, patterns persist.

The anxiety you carry is not random. It is the cost of absorbing impact meant for someone else.

Partnership or Project?

Look honestly.

Are you partnered? Or are you overseeing a long-term development project?

Does he initiate? Does he anticipate? Does he carry without being prompted? Or does he wait for direction?

You are not asking for perfection. You are asking for participation. And participation should not feel like pulling teeth.

Peace vs. Performance

Peace is not simply absence of conflict.

It is absence of vigilance. It is not having to monitor another adult. It is trusting that if you drop a ball, someone else will catch it.

If that has never been your experience, you may not realize how heavy vigilance is.

But once it lifts, you will feel the difference immediately. Anxiety drains quietly. Peace restores silently.

Reflection Prompts

- Where do you anticipate on his behalf?

- What responsibilities default to you without discussion?

- If you stopped reminding, what would happen?

- Do you feel relaxed in your own home?

- Are you partnered — or parenting?

The Truth Beneath It

You do not resent him for needing help. You resent him for refusing ownership.

You do not want to dominate. You want to share.

You do not want to control. You want to trust.

The anxiety of managing a grown man is not about superiority. It is about imbalance.

And imbalance erodes intimacy faster than conflict ever could.

Chapter 10

Sexual Obligation vs Sexual Autonomy

- Desire vs duty.

- Performance fatigue.

- The politics of access to women's bodies.

There is a silence around this subject.

Even among outspoken women. Even among feminists. Even among the "empowered." And even among best friends.

Because to admit it feels regressive.

But many women in long-term heterosexual relationships are not having sex because they are wildly, freely, joyfully desirous.

They are having sex because it feels required. Not overtly demanded. But structurally expected.

Sex has become maintenance.

And maintenance is not desire.

Desire vs. Duty

At the beginning, sex is electric. Anticipation. Curiosity. Mutual hunger.

There is choice in it. You lean in because you want to.

But over time, in unequal dynamics, something shifts.

You are tired. You are managing. You are carrying emotional labor. You are supervising logistics.

And then he reaches for you. Expectantly.

You hesitate. You weigh. Is this easier than explaining I'm exhausted? Is this simpler than navigating disappointment? Is this less work than another conversation?

And so you comply. Not dramatically. Not resentfully. Just... dutifully.

You tell yourself: It's normal. This is part of relationships.

He has needs.

And quietly, your own desire becomes secondary.

Call-Out – THIS IS CONDITIONING.

Women are taught that male sexual access within relationships is natural, expected, and stabilizing — while female desire is optional.

Performance Fatigue

Sex becomes performance when it is disconnected from authentic desire.

You know the choreography. The responsive sounds. The encouraging gestures. The strategic enthusiasm.

You are not faking entirely. You are participating. But participation is not the same as wanting.

And when sex becomes something you do to maintain harmony, it becomes labor.

Emotional labor was invisible. Sexual labor is embodied.

You begin to dread the initiation. Not because you dislike him.

Because you are depleted. And depletion kills desire faster than resentment.

And maybe you're a bit bored with it all. He's insatiable. Not again! you think. You push aside the desire to be doing other things with your precious time.

The Politics of Access

In many relationships, sex becomes proof of relational health.

If she declines often, something must be wrong. If he declines often, he must be stressed.

Notice the asymmetry.

A woman's refusal is a problem to be solved. A man's refusal is a circumstance to be respecte

Male libido is treated as baseline. Female libido is treated as negotiable.

So you manage it. You time your refusals carefully. You space them out. You compensate after conflict.

You become strategic about your own body.

Strategic. About access to yourself.

The "Blue Balls" Myth

Let us dismantle something quietly dangerous: The idea that men suffer physically if denied sex.

The implication that withholding is harmful. The subtle pressure that says: If you don't, you're being unfair.

No one dies from not having sex.

Desire is not an emergency. But the cultural narrative frames it as urgent.

This urgency places women in a position of gatekeeper. And gatekeeping breeds guilt.

You feel responsible for his frustration. You feel like the obstacle.

So you override your own hesitation. Again.

And again.

Sex as Emotional Regulation

In some relationships, sex becomes his primary way of reconnecting. After conflict, he initiates. After stress, he initiates. After distance, he initiates.

Sex becomes the glue. But glue cannot replace conversation.

And if emotional repair is replaced with physical access, something distorts.

You feel pressured to provide comfort through your body.

He feels soothed.

Nothing underlying is resolved.

You have offered intimacy. He has received regulation.

But your own needs remain suspended.

The Body Keeps Score

When sex is misaligned with desire, the body notices. Tension. Dryness. Discomfort. Fatigue.

You may not consciously resent it. But your body tightens. You begin to dissociate slightly. You go through the motions. You wait for it to end – his grand finale.

This is not trauma in the dramatic sense.

It is micro-erosion. A gradual separation from authentic desire.

The more often you override yourself, the harder it becomes to hear your own yes.

"But He Has Needs"

Yes.

So do you.

Desire is mutual or it is imbalanced.

If your needs are: Rest. Emotional safety. Shared responsibility. Respect. And those are not being met, why is sex prioritized?

You are told compromise is healthy.

But compromise around bodily access is not neutral.

When your body becomes bargaining chip for relational stability, autonomy shrinks.

Sex should be a shared expression. Not a pacifier.

Case Study: Maya

Maya was 42. Married for 15 years. Two children. Her husband was "a good man." Hardworking. Affectionate. Dependable financially.

She did not want sex most of the time. She was exhausted. She was jaded. She was bored with the routine of it all. There were other things she'd rather spend her time doing.

He interpreted her reluctance as rejection.

She began scheduling intimacy. Friday nights. Predictable. Efficient.

She would prepare mentally all day.

Afterwards, he felt close. She felt relieved it was over.

When she left the marriage years later, she was startled by something.

Her libido returned. Not instantly. But gradually.

In the absence of obligation, desire resurfaced.

It had not disappeared. It had been suppressed under pressure.

The Performance of Availability

Long-term partnership often assumes sexual continuity.

The expectation is not spoken daily. But it is there.

You feel it in the pauses. In the sighs. In the "we haven't in a while."

You begin to monitor frequency. You keep mental tallies.

You negotiate with yourself. This week was stressful. Maybe tomorrow. He seemed distant. Better tonight. We argued. This will smooth it.

Sex becomes currency. And currency changes the meaning of exchange.

Autonomy Is Erotic

Here is the paradox.

Desire thrives in autonomy.

When you feel free to say no, your yes becomes genuine.

When you feel safe declining, acceptance becomes enthusiastic.

But when refusal carries emotional consequence, consent becomes compromised. Not legally. Emotionally.

You may never say "I have to." But internally, you feel you should.

Should erodes desire.

The Myth of Maintenance Sex

Some relationship advice promotes "maintenance sex." The idea that frequency sustains connection.

But connection without authenticity is brittle.

If sex is happening while resentment simmers, the body associates intimacy with obligation.

Over time, aversion develops. Then panic. "Why don't I want him anymore?"

Often the answer is not mystery.

It is accumulation. Accumulation of unspoken fatigue. Accumulation of unequal labor. Accumulation of subtle pressure.

When You Stop

When a woman stops performing sexual availability, tension rises.

He may question:

"Are you not attracted to me?"

"Is there someone else?"

"Don't you care about our relationship?"

Rarely does he ask:

"Are you overwhelmed?"

"Are we sharing responsibilities?"

"Do you feel supported?"

Sex is treated as barometer.

But libido is responsive.

Responsive to safety. To fairness. To emotional connection.

If you are carrying the household and regulating emotions and shrinking ambition, desire does not flourish.

It withers.

Sexual Obligation as Emotional Tax

In unequal relationships, sex becomes one more task. One more way you maintain stability. One more thing you do to prevent friction.

It is not violent. It is draining. And draining intimacy hollows connection.

You begin to associate closeness with depletion. Which makes you withdraw further. Which increases his pursuit. Which increases your resistance.

A loop forms.

Reclaiming the Body

Sexual autonomy begins with a radical idea: Your body is not relational property. Even in marriage. Even in long-term commitment. Even when you love him.

Autonomy means:

You can decline without guilt.

You can initiate without obligation.

You can explore without performance.

You can rest without negotiation.

Autonomy is not weaponizing sex. It is removing it from barter.

The Fear Beneath It

Many women fear that asserting sexual autonomy will destabilize the relationship.

They are often correct.

Because if the relationship relied on access, removing assumed access reveals imbalance.

If sex was glue holding together emotional gaps, refusing maintenance exposes the cracks.

But cracks deserve examination. Not lubrication.

When Desire Returns

Women who leave unequal relationships often report a surprising phenomenon.

Desire returns in environments of safety. Not necessarily tied to a new partner. Sometimes alone. In privacy. In imagination. In self-touch.

When obligation disappears, curiosity revives.

Desire requires space. It cannot bloom under pressure.

The Radical Standard

Imagine this:

You only have sex when *you* genuinely want to. No strategy. No maintenance. No smoothing. Only desire.

How often would it happen?

Would the relationship survive that honesty?

If the answer is no, the problem is not your libido.

It is the structure.

Reflection Prompts

- When you say yes, is it enthusiastic or negotiated?

- Do you feel free to decline without consequence?

- Is sex connection — or conflict prevention?

- Does your body feel relaxed or braced during intimacy?

- If obligation disappeared, what would change?

The Final Line

Sex is not proof of love. Frequency is not proof of health. Access is not entitlement. Your body is not the price of partnership.

If intimacy costs you autonomy, it is too expensive.

And if peace requires sexual honesty, then honesty is sacred.

Because desire that is chosen is electric. Desire that is managed is exhausting.

Remember this: You were not built to be accessed. You were built to choose.

Chapter 11

The Slow Erosion of Self

- Identity diffusion.

- How women forget what they like.

- The quiet grief of becoming smaller.

No one wakes up one morning and says, "I think I'll disappear."

It doesn't happen like that.

There is no dramatic announcement. No visible fracture. No cinematic collapse.

The erosion is quiet. It happens in inches. In tone adjustments. In swallowed sentences. In postponed dreams. In careful calibrations of your personality to make someone else more comfortable.

You don't lose yourself in one catastrophic moment. You lose yourself in negotiations.

And most of them don't look like sacrifice at first. They look like love.

The First Compromise

It begins small. You laugh at a joke that bothers you. You agree to a plan you didn't want. You say, "It's fine," when it isn't.

Not because you're weak. Because you're flexible. Because you're generous. Because you understand relationships require give and take.

But if you track it honestly — how often are you giving? How often is he taking?

Erosion begins when compromise becomes one-directional.

The Recalibration of Personality

You are vibrant. You may be opinionated. Ambitious. Curious. Loud in your joy. Firm in your convictions.

Then you meet him.

At first, he says he loves your fire. Then he calls it "intense."

He loves your ambition — until it competes with his.

He loves your humor — until it outshines him socially.

He loves your intelligence — until it corrects him.

And so you adjust. Not consciously. You just... soften.

You speak a little less. You lead a little less. You downplay your accomplishments. You present yourself in ways that make him feel larger. You tell yourself it's maturity.

It isn't. It's self-editing.

The Art of Making Him Comfortable

You become fluent in his moods. You anticipate his insecurities before he voices them. You know when to shrink in public so he feels admired. You know when to praise him so he doesn't sulk. You know when to withhold your frustration so he doesn't withdraw.

You become an emotional translator. You say what he means more kindly than he can. You smooth over his social missteps. You buffer his temper. You explain his silence to your friends.

And somewhere in all of that labor, your interior world starts going unattended.

Because tending to yourself might disrupt him. And disruption feels dangerous.

The Gradual Silence

There is a particular ache that forms when you stop telling the truth in small ways.

You don't express disappointment anymore. You don't ask for more affection. You don't challenge dismissive comments. You don't initiate difficult conversations.

Because every time you did, it led to: Defensiveness. Withdrawal. Anger. The Silent Treatment. Punishment. Or worse — indifference.

So you decide peace is easier.

But peace built on suppression is not peace.

It is tension stored in the body. And it accumulates.

The Body Knows

Your mind can rationalize anything.

"He's just stressed."

"He didn't mean it."

"I'm overreacting."

"Relationships are hard."

But your body keeps score.

The tight jaw. The shallow breath. The insomnia. The low-grade anxiety. The constant mental rehearsal of how to say something without upsetting him.

You are not crazy.

You are compressed.

The Disappearing Friendships

Have you noticed this?

When a woman is slowly eroding, she sees her friends less.

Not always because he forbids it.

Sometimes because she is tired. Because she does not want to explain. Because she is embarrassed to admit how much she is tolerating. Because she fears her friends will see what she is trying not to see.

And so she isolates gently.

She tells herself she is "focused on the relationship."

But what she is really doing is reducing outside mirrors.

Because outside mirrors show you who you used to be. And that reflection can hurt.

The Career Contraction

Ambition shrinks in subtle ways.

You stop applying for opportunities that might disrupt his routine.

You don't pursue the promotion that requires relocation.

You don't start the business because his stability feels fragile.

You minimize your workload to preserve emotional energy for managing him.

And the world will call you "supportive." It will call you "balanced." It will call you "committed."

It will not call you what you are becoming: Smaller.

Gaslighting Yourself

The most insidious part of erosion is self-gaslighting.

You begin arguing against your own instincts.

When something feels wrong, you search for how it might be your fault. You police your tone before addressing his behavior. You critique your sensitivity instead of questioning his cruelty. You google relationship advice instead of recognizing imbalance. You assume you must need to communicate better, love harder, be more patient.

You rarely ask: Why does loving him require so much diminishment?

The Identity Shift

At some point, someone will say: "You've changed."

And you will bristle. Because you have.

You used to: Travel spontaneously. Speak boldly. Laugh louder. Take risks. Demand respect.

Now you: Check in constantly. Ask permission in subtle ways. Filter opinions. Prioritize harmony over authenticity.

You call it growth.

But growth does not feel like suffocation. Growth feels expansive.

If you feel smaller, that is not evolution. That is erosion.

Love Should Not Require Self-Abandonment

There is a lie women absorb early:

That love is proven by sacrifice.

Sacrifice sounds noble.

But what are you sacrificing? Time? Energy? Comfort?

Or identity?

There is a line between compromise and self-abandonment.

Compromise adjusts behavior. Self-abandonment edits personality.

If you would not recognize yourself five years ago, ask why.

The Emotional Climate

Some relationships function like unstable weather systems.

You become hyper-aware of atmospheric shifts. His tone changes — you notice. His energy dips — you compensate. His irritation spikes — you soothe.

You are always adjusting to prevent a storm.

Living like that trains your nervous system into vigilance. You cannot relax.

Because relaxation requires safety. And unpredictability is not safe.

When You Finally Speak

If you eventually gather the courage to express how diminished you feel, something predictable often happens.

He says: "I never asked you to do that."

Which is technically true. He didn't ask.

You adapted. You adapted to: Avoid conflict. Avoid rejection. Avoid emotional withdrawal. Avoid being labeled difficult.

The absence of explicit demand does not erase the environment that shaped your shrinking.

The Fear of Being "Too Much"

Many women begin eroding because they fear being too much.
Too emotional. Too ambitious. Too sexual. Too opinionated. Too needy.

But here is the quiet truth: You are rarely too much. You are simply too much for someone who benefits from you being less.

The right partner does not require reduction. He can handle amplitude.

The Moment of Realization

There is usually a moment.
It might be small.mYou hear yourself apologize for something that wasn't wrong. You watch him take credit for your idea. You see an old photo and feel grief for that woman. You sit in a room and realize you are performing yourself.

And something inside you whispers: This is not who I am.

Do not ignore that whisper.

It is the last intact piece of you trying to survive.

Why Leaving Feels Harder Than Staying

Erosion makes departure terrifying.

Because when you have shrunk, you doubt your ability to stand alone.

Your confidence is not where it used to be. Your financial independence may be weaker. Your social network thinner. Your sense of self blurred.

He becomes familiar terrain.

Even if it is uncomfortable terrain.

The unknown feels riskier than continued diminishment.

But here is the brutal truth: If you stay long enough, there will be less of you left to save.

Rebuilding the Self

If you recognize yourself in these pages, do not panic.

Erosion is slow.

But so is rebuilding.

Start with small reclamations. Say what you actually think in low-stakes conversations. Revisit an old hobby. Reconnect with a friend. Pursue a professional goal without apologizing.

Notice when you want to shrink — and don't.

The first time you resist self-editing will feel confrontational.

It isn't. It is alignment.

The Power Shift

Something interesting happens when a woman stops eroding.

She becomes unsettling.

Not because she is cruel. Because she is solid.

She no longer over-explains. She no longer anticipates every emotional fluctuation. She no longer absorbs blame reflexively. She no longer performs smallness.

This can destabilize a dynamic built on her reduction.

And sometimes the relationship will crack.

Let it. Anything that requires your disappearance to function is not sustainable.

Peace Versus Partnership

Remember the thesis of this book: *The Loneliness Lie and Why a Woman's Peace Outweighs Partnership.*

Peace is not the absence of a man.

Peace is the presence of yourself.

If partnership costs you your voice, your ambition, your humor, your rest, your authenticity — that is not companionship.

That is erosion disguised as love.

Loneliness is survivable.

Self-loss is not.

The Final Question

If you stripped away his preferences, his moods, his insecurities, his comfort — who would you be?

Are you still her?

If the answer is uncertain, that is your signal.

Not to explode. Not to accuse.

But to return.

Return to the parts you muted. Return to the dreams you deferred. Return to the voice you softened. Return to the body you ignored. Return to the friendships you sidelined.

Return to yourself.

Closing

The slow erosion of self does not make you weak.

It makes you human in a culture that rewards women for accommodating male fragility.

But you are not required to be sediment. You are not required to be shaped by someone else's current. You are not required to dissolve.

Stand.

Not loudly. Not angrily. Just fully.

And if standing fully costs you the relationship — let it cost.

Because the price of losing him is almost always lower than the price of losing yourself.

PART III: THE AWAKENING

When Peace Becomes More Attractive Than Partnership

The shift rarely arrives as a dramatic revelation. There is no thunderclap. No cinematic epiphany.

Instead, it begins quietly — almost imperceptibly — with a small and unsettling sensation: relief.

Relief when the phone does not ring. Relief when the argument ends. Relief when the house grows quiet and no one's moods need to be monitored.

At first, this relief can feel like guilt.

Because women are taught that partnership is the ultimate goal. That a relationship — even an exhausting one — is evidence of success. That wanting space is selfish. That wanting peace is suspicious.

So when calm begins to feel better than connection, the mind searches for explanations.

Maybe I'm being unfair. Maybe relationships are just hard. Maybe I expect too much.

But beneath those doubts, another realization slowly takes root — one that many women have been trained not to articulate.

I don't actually need this.

Not the conflict. Not the emotional caretaking. Not the endless negotiation required to maintain someone else's comfort.

This is the beginning of the awakening.

Not anger. Not rebellion.

Clarity.

The clarity that comes when a woman recognizes that solitude is not emptiness. It is space. Space to think. Space to breathe.mSpace to hear her own voice again after years of translating someone else's.

The chapters that follow trace this awakening — the quiet rediscovery of autonomy, the rebuilding of female networks, and the radical idea that fulfillment does not require male validation.

Because once a woman experiences peace without permission, the old scripts begin to sound very strange.

And once the script breaks, it is difficult to perform the role again.

Chapter 12

THE RADICAL IDEA: I DON'T NEED THIS

- Financial autonomy.

- Emotional independence.

- Community over coupledom.

There is a sentence that feels dangerous in a woman's mouth.

Not, "I don't want this." Not, "I deserve better." Not even, "I'm leaving."

The sentence that unsettles everything is quieter than that: ***I don't need this.***

Not him. Not the relationship. Not the validation. Not the status of being chosen.

Need is the currency that keeps many women compliant. Once need dissolves, control dissolves with it.

And a woman who does not need is a woman who negotiates differently. Or not at all.

The Fear of Not Needing

You were taught that interdependence is healthy. It is. But dependency disguised as romance is not.

There is a subtle cultural script that says: A woman should be capable — but not so capable she doesn't need a man.

Independent — but still longing. Self-sufficient – but still seeking completion.

When you say, even internally, "I don't need this,"you threaten a system that depends on your dependency.

And here is what makes it radical: It is not bitter. It is not angry. It is not anti-love.

It is grounded.

Financial Autonomy: The Unromantic Freedom

Let us begin where many women are uncomfortable being honest.

Money.

Financial autonomy is not about greed. It is about leverage.

If you cannot afford to leave, you are not *choosing* to stay. You are surviving. There is a difference.

For decades, women were told love conquers all.

But love does not pay rent. Love does not replace retirement contributions. Love does not fund your exit plan.

Financial autonomy changes your posture.

You speak differently when you know you can support yourself. You tolerate less when you are not economically cornered. You negotiate from preference, not fear.

This is not materialism. It is structural power.

The Myth of "He'll Take Care of Me"
Some women still internalize the fantasy: Find a stable man and you'll be safe.

But safety that depends on someone else's goodwill is not safety. It is conditional shelter.

What happens if he leaves? What happens if he cheats? What happens if he becomes resentful? What happens if he simply changes?

If your stability rests entirely on him, you are one decision away from destabilization.

Radical independence is not rejecting partnership. It is ensuring that partnership is additive, not essential for survival.

The Emotional Leverage of Money
There is something unspoken about financial dependence.

It silences.

You hesitate to push back. You soften your critiques. You avoid rocking the boat.

Not because you are weak. Because you are calculating risk.

Even if he never explicitly threatens you, the imbalance hums in the background.

The person who pays more often feels entitled to more say. More forgiveness. More tolerance. More control.

Financial autonomy quiets that hum. It removes the invisible hierarchy. It allows love to exist without economic intimidation.

Emotional Independence: The Inner Shift

Financial autonomy is external. Emotional independence is internal.

It is the moment you realize: I can survive his disappointment. I can survive his anger. I can survive his withdrawal. I can survive being misunderstood. I can survive being alone.

Many women stay in unsatisfying relationships not because they cannot pay bills — but because they fear emotional isolation. They fear being unchosen. They fear the silence. They fear the story others will tell about them.

Emotional independence begins when you accept:
Rejection does not annihilate you.
Loneliness does not erase you.
Solitude does not diminish you.

The End of Approval Addiction

There is a quiet addiction many women carry.

Male approval.

It can look subtle. Wanting to be desired. Wanting to be admired. Wanting to be validated. Wanting to feel special.

None of these are inherently wrong. But when approval becomes oxygen, you suffocate without it.

Emotional independence is when you like yourself without being liked.
When you respect yourself without being chosen.
When your worth does not fluctuate based on his mood.

That is radical.

Because it means he cannot control you with attention or its absence.

"But I Want Love"
Of course you do.

This chapter is not anti-love.

It is anti-*need*.

There is a difference between wanting a partner and requiring one for identity.

Wanting says: This would enhance my life.

Needing says: Without this, I am incomplete.

The radical idea is *not* that you will live alone forever. The radical idea is that if you did, you would still be whole.

Community Over Coupledom

Here is the quiet theft of modern culture: It elevates romantic partnership above all other bonds.

We are taught to prioritize: Husband over friends. Boyfriend over sisterhood. Marriage over community.

We relocate for men. We cancel plans for men. We reorganize lives around men.

And then, if the relationship ends, we find ourselves isolated.

Community is not a consolation prize. It is infrastructure. Friendship. Chosen family. Mentorship. Collaboration. Sisterhood.

These are stabilizing forces that outlast many romances.

When you build community intentionally, romantic partnership becomes one relationship among many — not the axis of your existence.

The Social Punishment

A woman who says, "I don't need this," will be labeled. Cold. Intimidating. Unrealistic. Too independent. Unfeminine. Bitter.

But examine who feels threatened by her autonomy:

Men who rely on female dependency for leverage.

Institutions that rely on marriage for social order.

Families that equate womanhood with partnership.

A woman who does not need a man cannot be coerced by fear of loneliness.

And that changes the bargaining table.

Redefining Security

Security is not a ring. Security is not shared rent. Security is not someone texting "goodnight."

Security is: Savings. Skills. Support networks. Self-trust. Emotional resilience.

If you lost him tomorrow, would you collapse — or recalibrate?

Radical independence aims for recalibration.

The Dating Shift

When you truly internalize "I don't need this," your dating behavior transforms.

You stop auditioning. You stop over-explaining. You stop ignoring red flags to avoid starting over. You stop lowering standards to secure attachment.

You evaluate compatibility from strength, not scarcity.

You are not trying to win. You are assessing.

And assessment unsettles men who prefer to be the evaluators.

The Inner Calm

There is a specific calm that comes from not needing.

It is not aloofness. It is steadiness.

You are not desperate for his next text. You are not rattled by minor inconsistencies. You are not panicked by temporary distance.

You are observing. Choosing. Participating.

But not clinging.

That energy changes dynamics immediately.

The Economic Reality

Let us speak plainly.

For many women, financial autonomy is harder than inspirational slogans suggest.

Wage gaps. Caregiving burdens. Career interruptions. Structural inequality.

This is not solved by mindset alone.

It requires planning. Skill-building. Negotiation. Career advancement. Investment literacy.

Radical independence is practical, not just emotional.

It is budgeting. It is learning. It is refusing to remain financially naive because "he handles that."

You handle it.

Even if you share responsibilities, you understand them.

Dependence thrives in ignorance. Power thrives in knowledge.

When He Senses the Shift

If you are in a relationship and begin embodying "I don't need this," he will notice.

Not because you threaten him overtly.

But because you stop chasing reassurance. You stop bending preemptively. You stop managing his comfort compulsively. You stop negotiating your boundaries internally before speaking them.

Some men will rise to meet this energy. Others will feel destabilized.

Their reaction will tell you everything.

The Freedom to Leave — or Stay

The ultimate power of not needing is this: You can stay because you want to. Not because you must.

That distinction changes love entirely.

When two people choose each other daily without dependency chains, the relationship is lighter. Cleaner. More honest.

If he stays, it is desire. If he leaves, it is survivable.

If you leave, it is not collapse. It is choice.

The Uncomfortable Truth

Here is what many women discover: The moment they stop needing, they become more desirable.

Not because they try harder. Because they radiate sufficiency.

There is something magnetic about a woman who is not negotiating from fear.

But do not adopt independence as a strategy to attract.

Adopt it as a philosophy of self-preservation.

Attraction is a side effect. Freedom is the goal.

The Identity Shift

Saying "I don't need this" is not about rejecting romance. It is about rejecting coercion.

It is about saying: I will not trade autonomy for access. I will not trade stability for proximity. I will not trade identity for attachment. I will not trade peace for partnership.

If partnership enhances peace, welcome it.

If it disrupts peace, release it.

That is radical. Because peace becomes the metric. Not relationship status.

The Final Reframe

For centuries, women's survival depended on attachment.

Today, in many parts of the world, survival is increasingly self-directed. The scripts have not caught up.

So when you choose independence, it feels rebellious.

It is.

But not because you hate men.

Because you love yourself enough to refuse dependency as destiny.

Closing

The radical idea is not that you will live alone.

The radical idea is that you could. And still be full. Still be supported. Still be loved. Still be safe. Still be powerful.

You do not need this relationship to validate your existence.

You do not need a partner to legitimize your adulthood.

You do not need male approval to confirm your worth.

If love comes, let it come freely.

If it goes, let it go without devastation.

Because the foundation is no longer him. It is you.

And a woman who does not need cannot be cornered.

She can only be chosen. Or walked away from.

And either way, she remains whole.

Chapter 13

Reclaiming Space

- Physical space.

- Mental space.

- Calendar space.

There is a moment after a woman stops shrinking, stops monitoring, stops needing — when she looks around and realizes something startling:

There is room. Room in her house. Room in her mind. Room in her calendar. Room in her body.

And she does not yet know what to do with it.

Because for years, space was not something she possessed. It was something she surrendered.

Reclaiming space is not loud. It is not dramatic.

It is quiet, deliberate, and deeply destabilizing to anyone who benefited from your contraction.

Space is power.

And this chapter is about taking it back.

Physical Space: The Geography of Autonomy
Start with the literal.

Walk through your home. What feels like yours?

Not shared. Not negotiated. Not approved.

Yours.

For many women, even in their own homes, space is conditional.

You adjust décor to avoid criticism. You rearrange furniture to accommodate preference. You pack away sentimental objects that he only sees as "clutter." You compress your belongings to make room for his.

You take up less square footage — subtly. A drawer becomes his. Then a closet. Then a room.

Your office becomes shared storage. You wish he'd find room in the garage for his golf clubs.

Your vanity shrinks or bears the remnants of this morning's shave.

Your books move to boxes.

None of this seems catastrophic.

But accumulation tells a story. Who expands? Who compresses?

Reclaiming physical space is the first visible rebellion. It is buying the chair you want. Hanging the art you love. Clearing the garage. Setting up the studio. Turning the spare room into your sanctuary instead of a symbolic mother-in-law's room.

It is not about aesthetics. It is about your territory.

The Body as Space
Your body is space, too.

Did you realize how often you folded yourself inward? Crossed your legs tighter. Lowered your voice. Made yourself physically smaller in rooms where male energy dominated.

Watch yourself now. Uncross your arms. Sit back. Stretch your legs.

Lean into the couch instead of perching.

You are allowed to inhabit your own frame fully.

There is something revolutionary about a woman who physically occupies space without apology.

Mental Space: The End of Intrusion
Physical space is visible. Mental space is harder to detect.

When you were in a relationship that required monitoring, a portion of your mind was always allocated to him.

Is he okay? Is he upset? Should I say something? Did I say too much? Why hasn't he responded? How do I phrase this carefully?

This constant mental tab never closed. It ran in the background like an app draining your battery.

Now, without him, something eerie but wonderful happens: Silence.

No mental rehearsal. No conflict simulation. No analysis of tone.

At first, your brain may still search for something to manage. Old habits die slowly.

But gradually, the mental real estate reopens. And with it comes clarity.

The Return of Concentration

Have you noticed how hard it was to focus before? To read deeply. To create. To think expansively.

When you are emotionally entangled in imbalance, cognition narrows.

Your mind is preoccupied with maintenance.

Now, reclaimed mental space allows you to think long-term again.

Ambition returns. Creativity sharpens. Ideas expand without interruption.

You are not dividing yourself between self and surveillance.

You are whole in your thinking.

That is no small shift.

The Unedited Thought

In a relationship where you shrank, even your thoughts were edited. You filtered internally before speaking externally. Eventually, you filtered before even forming conclusions.

Now, in reclaimed space, your thoughts roam uncensored.

You may think things that surprise you. Anger. Desire. Boldness. Clarity.

Let them surface. Reclaiming mental space means allowing the full spectrum of your interior world without self-policing.

Calendar Space: The Tyranny of Availability

Look at your calendar. How much of it used to orbit him? His schedule. His stress cycles. His family. His friends. His needs.

You rearranged your time to accommodate unpredictability. You kept evenings open "just in case." You avoided booking trips that might create tension. You left weekends flexible to prevent arguments about priority.

You were available.

Radical availability is not romantic. It is draining.

Reclaiming calendar space is not about being busy. It is about being intentional.

The Power of a Full Calendar

When you begin filling your calendar with your own priorities, something shifts.

Yoga class. Networking event. Dinner with friends. Solo travel. Professional development. Creative workshops.

You are no longer waiting to see what he wants. You are building a life that functions independently.

This does not mean you are anti-relationship. It means partnership must integrate into your schedule — not dominate it.

A woman with a life is not hard to love. She is just harder to control.

The Fear of Being "Unavailable"

Some women hesitate to reclaim calendar space because they fear appearing distant.

Men are often accustomed to women being elastic with time.

If you are no longer instantly reachable, instantly flexible, instantly responsive — some may test you.

"Why are you so busy?" "Don't you want to spend time together?" "You've changed."

Yes. You have. You are prioritizing your own architecture.

If someone feels threatened by your full life, that is diagnostic.

Not romantic.

Emotional Space: Not Everything Is Yours to Carry

Reclaiming space also means refusing emotional assignments you did not apply for.

You are not required to: Fix his trauma. Decode his silence. Absorb his rage. Translate his emotional illiteracy. Manage his friendships. Regulate his family dynamics.

Emotional space means drawing a perimeter.

His feelings are his responsibility. Your empathy does not equal obligation.

Compassion does not require absorption.

The Discomfort of Boundaries

When you begin reclaiming space, expect friction.

People accustomed to your elasticity will test your rigidity. They may call you selfish. Cold. Unavailable.

You are not. You are defined.

Boundaries feel aggressive only to those who benefited from your lack of them.

Stay steady.

The Relationship to Solitude

Reclaiming space requires comfort with solitude.

Not as punishment. Not as proof of independence. But as neutral ground.

Sit alone without filling the silence. Spend a weekend without social plans. Take yourself to dinner. Travel alone.

At first, this may feel performative. Then it becomes normal. Then it becomes powerful.

Solitude is not emptiness.

It is ownership.

The Reorganization of Energy

When you reclaim physical, mental, and calendar space, your energy reorganizes.

You are not scattered. You are directed. You are not reactive. You are proactive. You are not depleted.

You are strategic.

Energy once spent on monitoring and managing becomes available for growth.

And growth is intoxicating.

What Expands in New Space

When space opens, you must decide what fills it.

Old patterns will try to creep back in. Another Man Project. Another emotionally unavailable partner. Another dynamic that requires shrinking.

Be vigilant.

Do not refill reclaimed space with familiar dysfunction simply because it feels known. It took me three failed relationships after my one failed marriage to realise I was repeating the pattern.

Instead, experiment with expansion: Take the class. Launch the idea. Move cities. Invest boldly. Rest deeply.

Let your life stretch.

The Architecture of Self-Respect

Space is a structural expression of self-respect.

When you take up room physically, mentally, and temporally, you communicate something to yourself: I matter.

Not as a function of partnership. Not as an accessory to someone else's life. But as a primary character.

Reclaiming space is not about isolation. It is about centrality.

You are the center of your own existence. Not the supporting cast.

The Long-Term Vision

Imagine five years from now.

If you consistently protect your space, what grows? Financial security. Professional authority. Creative output. Stable friendships. Deep self-trust.

Now imagine five years of continued shrinking.

The contrast is stark.

Space determines trajectory.

Love After Space

Some women fear that reclaiming space will make them unlovable.

It does the opposite.

When you are not crowded by obligation and self-abandonment, you can offer love cleanly. You do not cling. You do not over-function. You do not negotiate your worth.

You invite partnership into a full life. Not into a vacuum.

That is magnetic.

The Quiet Confidence

There is a subtle shift when a woman occupies space unapologetically. She moves slower. Speaks clearer. Listens without scrambling. Chooses without urgency.

There is no rush to fill silence. No desperation to be selected.

She knows her time is valuable. Her mind is valuable. Her home is valuable. Her body is valuable.

And access is not automatic.

Closing

Reclaiming space is not loud activism.

It is daily architecture.

It is saying no without essay-length explanations.

It is leaving rooms that shrink you.

It is filling your home with objects that reflect you.

It is protecting your mornings.

It is scheduling your ambitions.

It is allowing your thoughts to roam without censorship.

It is taking up physical room.

It is refusing emotional clutter.

It is honoring your time as finite and precious.

You do not need to announce this shift. Just enact it.

Because once you reclaim space, something irreversible happens: You cannot comfortably shrink again.

The room feels too small. The silence feels too compromised. The calendar feels too crowded.

You have tasted expansion. And expansion ruins you for contraction.

That is not arrogance. It is alignment.

Take up room. In your house. In your mind. In your days. In your life.

And let anyone who feels displaced by that adjust accordingly.

Chapter 14

Female Friendship as Infrastructure

- Why women thrive in female networks.

- Interdependence without possession.

There is a lie women are fed so early we mistake it for oxygen: That romance is the structure of our lives. That a partner is the roof, the beams, the insulation, the electricity. That without him, we are exposed to the elements.

It is a beautiful story. It is also a fragile one.

Because the truth—quiet, unadvertised, unmonetized—is this: Women have always survived, thrived, endured, created, rebuilt, and risen inside female networks.

Not as accessories to men. But alongside one another.

Female friendship is not decorative. It is not a bonus tier unlocked after marriage. It is not the filler between romantic chapters.

Female friendship is infrastructure. It is plumbing. It is roads. It is the electrical grid.

And when you lose it—or neglect it—you discover very quickly how dark and cold life becomes.

This chapter is not sentimental. It is structural.

Because if women are going to live fully—whether partnered, single, widowed, divorced, child-free, or raising five children—we must understand something foundational:

Romance is optional. Community is not.

The Romance Pyramid Scam

We have been taught to build our lives like a pyramid. At the top: The One. Below him: Children. Below that: Work.

Somewhere near the bottom, like decorative stones: Friends.

Friends are treated as supplementary. Cute. Nice-to-have. Replaceable.

Until the relationship fractures. Until the husband travels constantly. Until the boyfriend leaves. Until the children grow up. Until illness strikes.

Until you are suddenly 47, in a quiet kitchen, realising the women you once texted daily have drifted away because you were "busy building your life."

You were building a pyramid. You forgot to build roads.

Men, as a group, are rarely socialised to provide emotional infrastructure. Many have friends, yes—but often activity-based. Parallel play. Shared hobbies. Low emotional labour.

Women are socialised differently. We are trained to notice. To remember. To check in. To sit in discomfort. To speak in nuance. To metabolise emotion.

We are, collectively, emotional architects. Yet we are encouraged to funnel those skills almost exclusively into romantic partnerships.

It is like hiring a team of civil engineers and asking them to decorate one house.

No wonder women feel underused and isolated. No wonder we burn out.

We were never meant to build only one thing.

The Ancient Blueprint

Historically, women did not live in nuclear isolation. They lived in compounds. Villages. Extended families. Shared courtyards.

They raised children collectively. Cooked collectively. Mourned collectively.

There were aunties, cousins, neighbours, widows, sisters.

No one woman was solely responsible for emotional weather control.

Then came the nuclear family. One man. One woman. One house. One primary emotional outlet.

The emotional load did not decrease. It concentrated.

Imagine taking an entire river system and rerouting it through a single pipe. Of course it bursts. Of course it corrodes. Of course the woman inside that house feels like she is drowning while smiling at dinner.

Female networks once absorbed shock. They offered perspective. They diluted intensity. They witnessed reality.

If a man was cruel, women whispered truth in kitchens. If he was kind, they celebrated it. If he died, they held the widow. If he left, they fed the children.

Community meant no single relationship determined survival.

When we lost that, we did not gain romance. We gained pressure.

Why Women Thrive in Female Networks

This is not an anti-man statement. It is a neurological and social observation.

Women, on average, are socialised toward relational processing. We are encouraged to articulate. To narrate. To contextualise. To emotionally translate.

In female friendship, this becomes reciprocal.

You say: "I'm tired." She hears the tone beneath the words. She asks the question beneath the sentence. She remembers what you said three months ago. She connects dots you forgot you drew.

There is mutual literacy.

With many male partners, emotional processing requires translation. With women, it often requires amplification.

This is not because men are incapable. It is because women have trained with one another since childhood.

Sleepovers are laboratories. Playground conversations are rehearsals. Teenage heartache debriefs are apprenticeships.

We learn how to sit in complexity together.

That skill does not evaporate at 30. It deepens.

Female friendship allows for layered identity. You can be messy. Brilliant. Angry. Tender. Ambitious. Jealous. Grieving. Hilarious.

And no one panics.

In romantic relationships, women often narrow themselves to maintain harmony.

In female networks, expansion is permitted. Encouraged. Celebrated.

Interdependence Without Possession

One of the most radical aspects of female friendship is this: It does not require ownership.

There is no expectation that one friend fulfils every need. There is no contract of exclusivity. No merging of bank accounts. No cultural script insisting: "You are incomplete without her."

You can have five close friends. Ten. Twenty acquaintances who show up when it matters.

Friendship allows for distributed reliance. One friend for intellectual sparring. One for laughter. One for practical help. One for grief. One for ambition.

The emotional ecosystem is diversified.

Romantic culture insists on concentration.

One partner must be: Lover. Best friend. Therapist. Co-parent. Financial collaborator. Sexual match. Social companion. Moral compass. Emergency contact.

It is a fantasy portfolio.

Friendship says: share the load.

Interdependence without possession is freedom. You depend on one another, yes. But you do not own one another. You do not police each other's time. You do not shrink each other's world. You do not feel threatened when she thrives. You expand with her.

The Myth of the Jealous Wife

Have you ever noticed how threatened some men are by strong female friendships?

"Why do you need to see them again?" "You tell them everything." "Don't you trust me?"

This is not about distrust. It is about decentralisation.

A woman with a strong network cannot be emotionally cornered. She has witnesses. Perspective. Validation. Support.

If something feels wrong, she has a sounding board.

Isolation is the soil in which control grows. Community is the light that prevents it.

When a woman maintains her friendships, she maintains her sanity. She maintains external calibration. She maintains narrative sovereignty.

That is not disloyalty. It is psychological hygiene.

Emotional Regulation as a Collective Act

When women gather, something extraordinary happens.

Emotion regulates. A problem spoken aloud becomes less catastrophic. A fear shared becomes less shameful. A joy celebrated becomes magnified.

This is not trivial. It is neurological.

Co-regulation lowers stress. Shared laughter releases tension. Physical proximity and eye contact reduce cortisol. Female friendship is preventative healthcare.

We pay therapists to provide what groups of women once gave freely around tables. Perspective. Mirroring. Challenge. Compassion.

This is not to diminish therapy. It is to recognise that women historically have been one another's emotional stabilisers.

Remove that, and women attempt to stabilise themselves alone.

Or lean entirely on a partner who may not possess the skillset.

Exhaustion follows.

Marriage as Emotional Monoculture

Monoculture farming is risky.

Plant one crop across miles of land and a single disease can destroy everything. Diversified crops are resilient.

Romantic culture encourages emotional monoculture. All eggs in one basket. All needs in one person.

When that relationship falters—even slightly—the emotional ecosystem collapses.

Women who maintain deep friendships experience shock differently.

There is grief, yes. But not annihilation.

There are hands. Chairs. Spare bedrooms. Emergency childcare. Financial advice. Moral clarity.

A network catches what one person cannot.

Infrastructure holds.

The Quiet Power of Witnessing

There is a specific kind of intimacy in female friendship that does not depend on performance.

She has seen you without mascara. Without certainty. Without composure.

She knows your history. Your patterns. Your mother's voice. Your worst decisions.

And she still sits beside you.

Romantic partners may love you. But often they met a curated version.

Friends saw the evolution. The before. The after. The in-between.

They are continuity. They hold your long narrative.

In a world obsessed with coupledom, female friends are archivists.

They remember who you were before compromise. Before accommodation. Before you convinced yourself you were "fine."

Sometimes, a single raised eyebrow from a long-time friend can dismantle an entire delusion. Not cruelly. Lovingly.

That is power.

When Women Drift

Here is the danger: Women often sacrifice friendships at the altar of romance. We disappear into relationships. We deprioritise girls' nights. We cancel brunches. We tell ourselves we are "busy."

Years pass.

The relationship strains.

We look up and realise we have neglected the very system that would have held us.

Rebuilding friendship requires humility. It requires admitting: "I withdrew."

Most women understand. Because they have done it too.

The tragedy is not that women prioritise love. It is that we are taught it must eclipse all else.

There is space for both. But only if we protect it deliberately.

Female Networks and Ambition

Women thrive in networks not only emotionally, but professionally.

Men have long leveraged old boys' clubs. Informal alliances. Mentorship pipelines.

Women, historically excluded from these spaces, built parallel ones.

Book clubs that become business incubators. WhatsApp groups that share job leads. Kitchen-table conversations that spark startups.

Female friendship often carries ambition without ego warfare.

Success is shared. Information is circulated. Opportunities are forwarded.

There is less scarcity thinking when the system is cooperative rather than competitive.

This is not utopian.

Women can be territorial. Tribal. Catty. Insecure.

But those behaviours flourish under patriarchy, where male validation is scarce currency.

Remove the scarcity. Remove the competition for proximity to power. Watch collaboration rise.

The Grief of Women Who Have None

There is a particular loneliness in women who lack female friendships.

They may be partnered. Surrounded by family. Financially stable.

And yet profoundly alone.

Because there is no one who understands the unedited interior. No one who speaks the shorthand. No one who can say, "Yes. Me too."

Romantic intimacy is not the same. Family love is not the same.

There is something about shared gendered experience that creates a specific bond.

Men cannot fully comprehend certain realities. The subtle fear walking at night. The quiet calculations in male-dominated rooms. The body memory of adolescence. The exhaustion of constant accommodation.

When women speak these truths to one another, there is relief.

Not explanation. Recognition.

Interdependence Without Collapse

Critics of female networks sometimes sneer: "Sounds codependent."

It is not.

Codependence is fusion without boundaries. Female friendship, at its healthiest, is connection with autonomy.

You can disagree. Disappear for weeks. Pursue separate lives. Love different men. Vote differently. Parent differently.

And still remain anchored.

There is elasticity.

Romantic culture often confuses intensity with depth.

Friendship offers depth without constant intensity. It allows ebb and flow. You can be in crisis and receive support. You can be steady and offer it.

Roles shift. Balance restores. No one is permanently cast as rescuer or rescued.

That fluidity is strength.

The Radical Idea

Here is the radical idea at the heart of this chapter: A woman does not need to derive her primary emotional sustenance from a romantic partner.

She can distribute it.

She can build a network so strong that no single departure destroys her. She can be partnered and still anchored elsewhere. She can be single and richly connected. She can age surrounded by women who know her story.

Infrastructure is built slowly. Deliberately. Brick by brick. Text by text. Dinner by dinner.

It requires showing up when nothing dramatic is happening. It requires consistency over spectacle.

Romance thrives on intensity. Friendship thrives on reliability.

One is fireworks. The other is electricity.

Which keeps the lights on?

The First Time You Feel It

There is a moment many women experience after leaving a draining relationship.

The first quiet dinner with friends. The first laugh that comes from the belly, not politeness. The first time someone says, "We've missed you."

You realise how small you had become. How narrow your world. How carefully you curated your availability.

In that moment, something widens. Air returns. Colour returns.

You are not being evaluated. You are not monitoring anyone's mood. You are not adjusting your tone. You are simply present.

Female friendship is oxygen. You do not notice its absence until you breathe deeply again.

Building It Intentionally

If female friendship is infrastructure, it must be maintained. Reach out. Invite. Host. Attend.

Be the one who remembers birthdays. Be the one who checks in. Be the one who says, "Are you really okay?"

This is not martyrdom.

It is investment.

And choose wisely.

Not every woman is safe. Not every group is nourishing.

Look for reciprocity. For growth. For humor. For honesty without cruelty. For support without possession. Infrastructure built from unstable materials collapses.

Choose brick, not cardboard.

Ageing and Female Networks

As women age, female friendship becomes even more critical. Children leave. Careers shift. Bodies change. Parents die.

Romantic relationships may endure—or end.

The women who have cultivated networks enter later life buffered. They have walking companions. Travel companions. Medical advocates. Witnesses to decades.

Widowhood is devastating. But widowhood inside community is survivable.

Illness is terrifying. But illness inside network is manageable.

Loneliness kills. Community sustains.

The End of the Fairy Tale

The fairy tale ends with marriage.

Real life begins after.

What if the true story women need is not about finding one person who completes us — but about building a constellation.

What if fulfilment is not fusion — but connection across many points?

What if the goal is not possession — but participation?

Female friendship is not the consolation prize. It is not what remains if romance fails. It is not the side dish.

It is the table. It is the ground. It is the wiring beneath the walls. It is the invisible system that keeps everything else functioning.

You can choose romance. You can choose marriage. You can choose solitude.

But whatever you choose, build your network.

Invest in women. Show up. Be seen. Witness and be witnessed.

Because when the lights flicker, when the storm comes, when the story shifts — it will not be the fairy tale that saves you.

It will be the infrastructure.

And women, when we remember who we are to one another, build beautifully.

Chapter 15

Redefining Success

- Partnership as optional.

- Fulfillment without male validation.

- Choosing peace as the metric.

There is a question women are asked, implicitly or explicitly, from girlhood onward:

"But have you met someone?"

It is delivered at family gatherings. At graduations. At weddings. At job promotions. At housewarmings. Even at funerals.

You can earn degrees, publish books, build companies, travel the world, buy property, raise children alone, recover from heartbreak, heal from trauma, run marathons, survive illness — and still, the evaluation hovers:

"Yes, but... have you found someone?"

Male partnership has been positioned as the final audit. As though every achievement remains provisional until endorsed by a man.

It is a quiet hierarchy. Romance at the top. Everything else below.

This chapter dismantles that hierarchy.

Not to discourage partnership. But to remove its monopoly on meaning.

Success must be redefined — not in defiance, not in bitterness — but in clarity.

Because when you define success incorrectly, you build your life around the wrong metric.

And women have been measuring themselves against a flawed ruler for generations.

The Old Metric

Under the old system, a woman's success followed a predictable arc: Be desirable. Be chosen. Be kept. Be envied.

If she achieved professional success but was single, there was a caveat.

If she was beautiful but unmarried, there was speculation.

If she was powerful but divorced, there was analysis.

If she was accomplished but child-free, there was suspicion.

A man's life expands with achievement. A woman's life is cross-examined.

The question beneath it all is ancient: "Is she validated?"

And validation, historically, meant male approval. Male desire. Male presence. Male commitment.

Remove that, and a woman's life is considered unfinished. Incomplete.

This narrative has been so persistent that even fiercely independent women internalise it.

They achieve everything — and still feel the phantom deficit.

The absence of a partner becomes louder than the presence of accomplishment.

This is not accidental. It is cultural conditioning.

Partnership as Optional

Let us begin here: Partnership is beautiful when it is healthy. *But it is not mandatory.*

Not for survival. Not for identity. Not for legitimacy.

Partnership is a choice. A meaningful one, yes. But optional.

Optional means:
Your life can be complete without it.
Your days can be full without it.
Your future can be stable without it.

Optional means you are not waiting in the lobby of your own life.

You are not on pause.
You are not in rehearsal.

Optional means you are not deficient.

You are simply unpaired.

There is a profound psychological shift when a woman moves from "I hope someone chooses me" to "If someone joins me, it will be because they enhance what is already whole."

That shift removes desperation. And desperation distorts standards.

When partnership is mandatory, women tolerate misalignment.

When partnership is optional, women assess compatibility calmly.

Optionality restores power.

The Fear Narrative

Why does this idea provoke such resistance?

Because women are fed a fear narrative. You will be lonely. You will regret it. You will be pitied. You will miss out. You will become bitter.

You will die alone.

Notice what is rarely included in this warning:
You may be peaceful.
You may be free.
You may be deeply connected to friends.

You may build something extraordinary.
You may wake each day without emotional tension.
You may discover yourself fully.

The fear narrative exists because independence destabilises control structures.

A woman who does not require male partnership cannot be coerced by the threat of its absence.

She cannot be rushed. She cannot be shamed into settling. She cannot be manipulated with scarcity.

Optionality is threatening to systems that rely on urgency.

Fulfillment Without Male Validation
Validation is addictive. It always has been.

To be seen. Praised. Desired. Chosen.

There is nothing inherently wrong with enjoying male attention.

The issue arises when it becomes the primary source of self-worth.
When beauty feels urgent.
When ageing feels catastrophic.
When rejection feels annihilating.
When silence feels like invisibility.

If your reflection depends on male eyes, you will constantly adjust your posture. Your tone. Your ambition. Your opinions.

You will shrink when necessary. Soften when required. Laugh when unamused. Nod when unconvinced.

Because the reward is approval. But approval is conditional. And conditional validation is exhausting.

Fulfillment without male validation is not about rejecting men. It is about relocating the mirror.

Your work reflects you. Your friendships reflect you. Your integrity reflects you. Your body reflects your lived experience, not your market value. Your peace reflects your standards.

When the mirror moves inward, something steadies. You become less reactive. Less anxious. Less performative.

There is no audience to impress. There is only a life to inhabit.

The Performance of Femininity

For generations, women have performed femininity as strategy. Smile more. Argue less. Be agreeable.

Be desirable but not intimidating.
Be ambitious but not threatening.
Be intelligent but not condescending.
Be independent but still "easy."

This balancing act consumes energy.

Women learn to edit themselves before entering rooms. To calculate reactions. To predict male discomfort.

The performance is subtle but constant.

When male validation ceases to be the primary goal, the performance softens.

You stop adjusting your laugh. You stop modulating your opinions to remain attractive. You stop fearing that success will make you unlovable.

Because love, if it arrives, must adapt to you — not the other way around.

That is fulfillment. Living unedited.

Choosing Peace as the Metric

If partnership is optional and validation is internal, what becomes the measure of success?

Peace.

Not the Instagram version. Not the curated aesthetic. But genuine, nervous-system-level peace.

The absence of chronic anxiety. The absence of emotional volatility. The absence of walking on eggshells.

Peace means your home is not tense. Your phone does not trigger dread. Your evenings are not spent analysing tone. Your body is not braced for conflict.

Peace is underrated because it is quiet.

Drama is cinematic. Peace is stable.

But stability is fertile ground.

In peace, creativity returns. Energy returns. Clarity returns.

A woman at peace is not bored. She is grounded.

Choosing peace as the metric means asking a different question: Does this relationship expand my calm? Or does it erode it?

Does this ambition energise me? Or exhaust me for external applause?

Does this lifestyle reflect my values? Or my fear of being left behind?

Peace is not laziness. It's alignment.

The High-Achieving Woman's Trap

There is a specific trap for capable women.

They achieve professionally. They maintain homes. They manage families. They cultivate friendships. They look composed.

And still, internally, they chase male approval.

They date men who underperform emotionally. They overfunction. They tolerate ambiguity.

Because the subconscious belief remains: "If I can succeed at everything else, surely I can succeed at love."

Love is not a performance metric. It is a mutual exchange.

When partnership is treated like an exam to pass, women exhaust themselves proving worthiness.

Optionality ends the exam.

You are not trying out. You are evaluating.

And evaluation is calmer than auditioning.

The Cultural Panic Around Single Women

Notice how society reacts to single men versus single women.

The single man is independent. Focused. Career-driven.

The single woman is questioned. Is she too picky? Too career-obsessed? Too damaged? Too intimidating?

The assumption is that something must explain her singleness. Because partnership is presumed natural.

This presumption is outdated.

Women now have economic autonomy. Educational access. Property ownership. Reproductive choice. Mobility.

The original structural reasons for compulsory marriage have shifted.

Yet the psychological narrative lingers.

Redefining success requires refusing that narrative.

You do not owe anyone an explanation for your autonomy. You do not need to soften it to be palatable.

The Economics of Peace

Financial autonomy is part of this equation.

When a woman can support herself, partnership shifts from necessity to preference.

This changes everything.

She is not calculating survival. She is calculating compatibility.

Peace is easier to choose when you are not financially cornered.

This is not romantic. It is practical.

Women who can afford their own lives can afford to walk away. And the ability to walk away is power.

Power does not guarantee solitude.

It guarantees choice.

Fulfillment in Multiplicity

Fulfillment does not require a single source. It can be layered.
Work that stimulates.
Friends who sustain.
Family that anchors.
Solitude that restores.
Travel that expands.
Art that expresses.
Community that supports.

Romance, if it fits, that complements.

The danger of elevating partnership above all else is narrowing.

When one role dominates identity, its absence feels catastrophic.

When identity is diversified, loss is painful but not annihilating.

This is not cynicism. It is resilience.

The Peace Test

Here is a simple test for redefining success:

Imagine your life five years from now.

Remove the image of a partner.

Is there still richness? Activity? Connection? Purpose?

If the answer is no, that is not because partnership is mandatory. It is because you have not yet built a full independent ecosystem.

Build that. Not as rebellion. But as foundation.

Then, if someone joins, they join abundance. Not vacancy.

The Quiet Confidence of Optional Women

There is something unmistakable about a woman who knows partnership is optional.

She is not hardened. She is not cynical. She is steady.

She does not oversell herself. She does not chase attention. She does not collapse at mixed signals.

She listens. She observes. She chooses slowly.

Her energy is not frantic. Because she is not bargaining with loneliness.

Loneliness may visit. But it does not terrify her.

She has community. Purpose. Self-trust.

This calm is magnetic. Not because she performs it. But because it is genuine.

Redefining the Endgame

For decades, the endgame presented to women was marriage. White dress. Ring. Photographs. Applause.

But marriage is not an endgame.

It is a dynamic state requiring continuous work.

Some marriages thrive. Some endure. Some erode. Some end.

If marriage is the peak, what happens when it fails?

Redefining success means detaching from static milestones.

Instead, success becomes fluid.

Am I aligned? Am I at peace? Am I growing? Am I connected? Am I respected?

These questions can be asked whether single, partnered, divorced, widowed, dating, or uninterested.

The metric is internal stability, not external optics.

Ageing Without Panic

When male validation is the primary metric, ageing becomes crisis.

When peace is the metric, ageing becomes transition.

Wrinkles are not rejection. They are evidence.

The female body shifts. So does ambition. So does desire.

A woman who measures success by male attention will experience ageing as loss.

A woman who measures success by peace experiences ageing as evolution.

She may still desire romance. But she does not panic at its fluctuations.

Because her identity is not collapsing with each birthday.

The Unlearning

Redefining success is not instantaneous.

It requires unlearning. Unlearning the fairy tales. Unlearning the comparison. Unlearning the subtle shame.

It requires noticing when you feel "behind."

Behind whom? According to which script? Says who?

Often, the anxiety dissolves under scrutiny.

The timeline was inherited. It was conditioned. Not chosen.

Peace Is Not Settling

There is a misunderstanding that choosing peace means settling for less.

It does not.

It means refusing chaos disguised as passion. Refusing volatility disguised as chemistry. Refusing anxiety disguised as excitement.

Peace does not eliminate intensity. It anchors it.

A healthy partnership can be passionate and peaceful. Ambition can be ambitious and peaceful. Friendship can be lively and peaceful.

Peace is not the absence of life. It is the absence of chronic threat.

Women who have experienced relational turbulence know this difference viscerally.

The body recognises safety.

And once you have tasted it, you are less willing to abandon it for spectacle.

The Final Reframe

Success is not: Being chosen. Being envied. Being admired. Being married.

Success is: Being aligned. Being calm. Being connected. Being self-respecting.

Being free to choose — and to leave.

Partnership may be part of that life. It may not.

But it is no longer the crown. It is a companion possibility.

When women redefine success this way, something radical happens. We stop bargaining with ourselves. We stop shrinking to qualify. We stop measuring our worth by proximity to men.

We build lives that feel whole from the inside.

And if someone joins that life, it is not because we were incomplete. It is because we were open.

Open is different from empty. Open is strength. Empty is hunger.

The old metric fed hunger. The new metric feeds peace.

And peace, once chosen deliberately, becomes addictive in the healthiest way.

Because when you wake up unafraid, unbraced, unedited—

When your life is yours, fully—

You realise something extraordinary: You were never behind. You were simply measuring with the wrong ruler.

Redefine it.

And watch your entire life recalibrate.

PART IV: THE EXIT

Leaving Without Apology

What happens when a woman stops negotiating with her own peace.

For most of this book, we have examined the architecture of staying.

The quiet bargains. The emotional labor. The slow narrowing of a woman's life in order to maintain a relationship that asks more than it gives.

Part I exposed the mythology — the stories women are taught about love, sacrifice, and partnership as destiny.

Part II took inventory of the cost — the invisible taxes paid in time, energy, self-editing, and exhaustion.

Part III was the realization – the "I don't need this".

By now, a pattern should be unmistakable: many women are not failing at relationships. They are *overperforming* in them.

They are stabilizing systems that were never balanced to begin with.

Part IV begins where the internal shift happens.

Not the dramatic exit people imagine. Not the cinematic breakup speech or the slammed door.

The real exit begins much earlier and far more quietly. It begins the moment a woman stops negotiating with her own peace.

The moment she notices that the silence after conflict feels like relief.

The moment she realizes that solitude is not the threat she was taught to fear.

The moment she asks a question that destabilizes everything that came before: What if leaving is not failure — but clarity?

This section traces the emotional arc of that realization. The guilt. The recalibration. The rediscovery of space, autonomy, and self-trust.

Because once a woman stops organizing her life around the maintenance of someone else's comfort, something remarkable happens.

Her life begins to expand again.

And expansion, once tasted, is very hard to surrender.

Chapter 16

THE GUILT SCRIPT

- "You're giving up."

- "You'll regret it."

- "I'm the best you can do"

- "Good luck finding someone better."

There is a moment that comes when a woman begins to detach. Not loudly. Not theatrically. Not in the cinematic way that movies like to imagine, with slammed doors and triumphant music swelling in the background.

In real life, it is quieter than that.

It begins as a thought she does not immediately voice. A subtle shift in her internal weather. A realization that lands softly but refuses to leave.

I do not have to stay.

That thought is revolutionary.

And revolutions, even small personal ones, provoke resistance.

But almost immediately, the scripts begin.

They are not new scripts. They have existed for generations. They have simply been passed down, rehearsed, refined. Mothers whisper them. Friends repeat them. Men deploy them with remarkable confidence. Society echoes them until they sound like wisdom.

They are the Guilt Script.

And like any script, they rely on the woman playing her assigned role.

When she refuses, the performance falters.

But the lines keep coming.

"You're Giving Up."
This is often the first accusation. It arrives disguised as disappointment.

The phrase implies something deeply moral: that perseverance is virtuous and departure is weakness.

But notice what is being reframed.

Leaving an unhealthy dynamic is not giving up. It is refusing to continue investing energy into something that has shown no interest in growth.

Yet the script insists that endurance equals virtue.

Women are taught this lesson early. Be patient. Be understanding. Be forgiving. Relationships take work.

All of which sounds reasonable until you examine the distribution of that work.

In many heterosexual relationships, the labor of maintenance falls disproportionately on women. She manages the emotional temperature. She smooths over conflicts. She absorbs frustration. She anticipates needs.

If the relationship struggles, she is told to try harder. If the relationship fails, she is told she gave up too soon.

What is rarely asked is whether the structure itself was sustainable.

Imagine telling someone who has been holding up a collapsing ceiling with their bare hands for years that they are weak for finally stepping aside.

"You're giving up."

No. She is simply refusing to continue being the load-bearing beam.

And the remarkable thing is that once she steps away, the structure often collapses instantly. Which tells you everything about who was holding it up.

Perseverance as a Female Virtue

There is a cultural myth that women are uniquely suited to suffering nobly.

Stories celebrate the long-suffering wife. The patient girlfriend. The woman who stands by her man while he "works through things."

Her endurance is portrayed as proof of her depth. But endurance without reciprocity is not devotion. It is depletion.

A woman who stays too long is praised for her loyalty. A woman who leaves is accused of impatience. Cruelty. Being overly emotive.

The line between loyalty and self-abandonment is rarely discussed. Because if women began examining that line honestly, many relationships would end far sooner.

The guilt script relies on this confusion. It reframes departure as failure rather than discernment.

"You're giving up." The implication is that success means staying indefinitely.

Even if the cost is yourself.

"You'll Regret It."
This line carries a prophetic tone.

It suggests that the woman is making an impulsive decision she will later mourn.

The future is invoked like a courtroom witness. One day, the script warns, you will wake up alone and wish you had stayed. The fear of regret is powerful because humans are wired to avoid loss.

But the script carefully ignores another possibility.

She might regret staying. In fact, many women do.

They regret the years spent managing someone else's emotions. The ambitions they quietly shelved. The friendships neglected. The opportunities postponed.

Regret is not exclusive to those who leave. It is also common among those who stayed far longer than they should have.

Yet the cultural narrative rarely explores that side of the equation.

There are countless stories warning women about the regret of solitude. There are far fewer stories about the regret of self-erasure.

And yet if you speak privately with women in their fifties, sixties, seventies, a pattern often emerges. Some will tell you that they are grateful for the lives they built. Others will quietly admit that they lost themselves in the process.

The guilt script depends on keeping those conversations hidden.

The Myth of the Regretful Woman

Popular culture is obsessed with the image of the woman who leaves and then suffers for it. She is portrayed as lonely. Bitter. Punished by time.

Meanwhile, men who leave relationships are often portrayed as independent, adventurous, even admirable.

He is rediscovering himself. She is making a mistake. The asymmetry is striking.

But reality is less tidy than these narratives. Many women who leave describe a different emotion entirely.

Relief.

Not dramatic joy. Not immediate bliss. Just relief.

Relief from monitoring someone else's moods. Relief from constant negotiation. Relief from the low-grade anxiety of wondering when the next conflict will arrive.

This relief can feel disorienting at first. Women who have spent years managing a relationship often experience silence as unfamiliar.

The nervous system, accustomed to vigilance, takes time to recalibrate. But gradually, the quiet begins to feel like oxygen.

And regret, so confidently predicted by the guilt script, fails to materialize.

"I'm the Best You Can Do."
This line is less subtle.

Sometimes it is stated directly. Sometimes it is implied. It rests on a devastating assumption: that the woman's value in the dating market is fragile, diminishing, precarious.

Men are told their desirability increases with age. Women are told theirs declines.

This belief is repeated so often that it begins to sound like biological fact. But much of it is cultural mythology.

It is convenient mythology, of course. If a woman believes that leaving means she will never find another partner, she is far less likely to leave. Fear is an effective containment strategy.

And so the script encourages her to view her current partner as her final opportunity.

"Better the devil you know..." Take this deal, the message goes. There may not be another.

Scarcity Thinking

Scarcity is one of the most powerful psychological forces.

When people believe resources are limited, they cling more tightly to what they have.

The guilt script deliberately frames partnership as scarce.

Good men are rare. You're lucky to have one. Don't be too picky.

These phrases appear reasonable on the surface. But they often conceal a deeper instruction:

Lower your standards.

Accept less.

Be grateful.

The woman is encouraged to view the relationship not through the lens of fulfillment but through the lens of scarcity.

He may not be ideal, the logic goes, but at least he is something. And something, in a scarcity framework, always seems better than nothing.

But this reasoning ignores a crucial variable: Peace.

A life without chronic emotional strain is not "nothing." It is something profound.

And many women discover this only after leaving relationships that demanded constant compromise.

The Negotiation of Worth

"I'm the best you can do" is not merely an insult.

It is a negotiation tactic. It attempts to redefine the woman's perceived value.

If she believes she cannot do better, she will tolerate more. More disrespect. More emotional labor. More imbalance.

The script works only if she accepts the premise.

But the premise itself is rarely interrogated. Who defines what "better" means?

Is better someone with a higher income? A more charming personality? A more attractive face?

Or is better someone who contributes equally to emotional stability? Someone who respects boundaries. Someone who does not require constant management.

When women begin redefining "better" in terms of peace rather than prestige, the script loses much of its power.

Because suddenly the comparison is not between two men. It is between a man and a life of autonomy.

And that is a much harder competition.

"Good Luck Finding Someone Better."

This line is often delivered with a hint of sarcasm.

It carries the same underlying message as the previous script but adds an element of mockery.

The woman's expectations are portrayed as unrealistic. Her standards are ridiculed.

The implication is that she is naïve, perhaps even arrogant, to believe she deserves more.

This tactic is particularly effective because women are socialized to avoid appearing demanding. A woman who asks for too much risks being labeled difficult.

So the script pressures her to retreat. To apologize for wanting more. To shrink her expectations until they fit the relationship available.

The Punishment for Standards

One of the most revealing social experiments occurs when a woman raises her standards.

She asks for emotional reciprocity. She asks for accountability. She asks for respect.

Rather than inspiring improvement, these requests often provoke defensiveness.

The requests themselves are framed as unreasonable. You're asking for too much. You're impossible to please. No man will put up with that.

Notice the rhetorical move.

Instead of addressing the request, the script attacks the woman's expectations.

Her standards become the problem. Not the behavior she is responding to.

This reversal is powerful because it redirects the conversation away from the actual issue. The relationship does not need to change. The woman does.

The Social Chorus

The guilt script is rarely delivered by men alone.

It often appears in the voices of friends, relatives, coworkers.
"Are you sure you want to throw this away?"
"Relationships aren't perfect."
"You might not find someone else."

These comments are usually offered with genuine concern. But concern can still reinforce harmful narratives.

Many people are deeply invested in the idea that partnership is the ultimate marker of success. When someone challenges that idea, it unsettles the collective belief system.

If she can walk away, what does that say about the compromises everyone else has made?

The easiest response is to encourage her to stay.

Not because staying is best for her, but because it preserves the social script.

The Fear of Female Autonomy

At its core, the guilt script reflects a deeper anxiety.

A woman who no longer fears being alone is difficult to control.

Traditional relationship dynamics often rely on asymmetry.

If one partner fears departure more than the other, the balance of power tilts.

Historically, women had more to lose from leaving. Economic dependence, social stigma, legal barriers.

Those structures have weakened in many places, but their psychological echoes remain.

The guilt script attempts to restore the old asymmetry. It reminds the woman, again and again, that leaving carries consequences.

Loneliness.

Regret.

Scarcity.

These consequences are presented as inevitable. But inevitability is rarely examined.

The Quiet Rebellion

What happens when the script fails?

Something surprisingly quiet. The woman stops arguing. She stops defending her decision. She stops trying to convince others that her reasoning is valid.

Instead, she simply proceeds.

This quiet refusal is deeply disruptive.

The guilt script expects engagement. It expects the woman to debate, to justify, to explain.

When she declines to participate, the script loses its audience.

And without an audience, scripts collapse.

Rewriting the Narrative

Rejecting the guilt script does not mean rejecting relationships. It means rejecting the idea that relationships must be preserved at any cost.

It means recognizing that leaving can be an act of discernment rather than failure.

It means understanding that regret is not the exclusive domain of those who walk away.

Most importantly, it means redefining success.

Success is not measured by the duration of a partnership. It is measured by the quality of a life.

A partnership that enhances that life is welcome. A partnership that erodes it is optional.

This is the radical idea that unsettles the guilt script.

Because if women truly internalize it, the old pressure mechanisms lose their effectiveness. Fear stops working. Scarcity stops working. Mockery stops working.

And once those tools fail, the only thing left is genuine partnership. Not coerced partnership. Not guilt-driven partnership. But partnership freely chosen.

The End of the Script

There will always be voices that attempt to revive the old lines.

"You're giving up."

"You'll regret it."

"I'm the best you can do."

"Good luck finding someone better."

But once a woman has seen the script clearly, it becomes difficult to unsee.

The lines sound rehearsed. Predictable. Almost boring in their familiarity.

And the power they once held begins to dissolve.

Because the most dangerous thing a woman can do in the face of the guilt script is remarkably simple.

She can refuse the role. She can step off the stage.

And she can walk into a life that no longer requires apology.

Chapter 17

The First Quiet Night Alone

- The most painful step, followed by the euphoria of relief

- Relief disguised as guilt.

- The absence of emotional monitoring.

There is a night no one prepares you for.

Not the night you leave. Not the night you pack. Not the night of the final argument.

The first quiet night alone.

The door closes. The house settles. Your phone is still.

And for the first time in a long time — no one's mood is in the room with you.

No one is irritated. No one is demanding, withdrawing, sulking or waiting to be managed.

Just you. And silence. And something unexpected.

Relief.

Followed immediately by guilt.

The Relief You Weren't Supposed to Feel

You were supposed to feel shattered. Devastated. Regretful. Terrified.

Lonely.

That's what the scripts say.

You ended a relationship. You should be grieving.

And you are grieving. But beneath the grief, there is something else.

Your shoulders drop. Your breath deepens. You notice the absence of tension you had stopped noticing.

No one is about to walk through the door with a storm on his face. No one needs debriefing. No one requires careful tone management. No one needs you to interpret their silence. You don't have to interpret yours.

You can exhale.

And the exhale feels almost sinful. Because if he mattered, shouldn't you be wrecked?

Here is the truth no one tells you: Relief does not negate love. It exposes burden.

The End of Emotional Monitoring

When you lived with him, your nervous system was on shift. Constantly.

You didn't call it anxiety. You called it "being attentive."

You didn't call it vigilance. You called it "being supportive."

You didn't call it emotional labor. You called it "partnership."

But what you were doing was monitoring. Monitoring his tone. Monitoring his facial expressions. Monitoring how tired he looked. Monitoring whether he seemed distant. Monitoring how much praise he needed that day. Monitoring whether tonight was safe for a difficult conversation.

It was subtle. You did it automatically.

You didn't even realize how much bandwidth it consumed. Until it stopped.

That first night alone, you reach for the invisible dashboard. There are no gauges to read. No barometers to check. No temperature shifts to predict. It is disorienting.

And so liberating.

The Quiet Is Not Lonely

There is a difference between silence and absence. Silence is spacious. Absence is hollow.

That first night, you expect hollowness. Instead, you find space. You sit on the couch and no one is reacting to what you're watching. You eat dinner without calibrating portions or preferences. You go to bed without negotiating temperature, timing, intimacy, or resentment.

You leave a light on. Or you don't. You play music. Or you don't.

No one sighs. No one comments. No one withdraws. No one grunts, farts, picks their toenails.

The quiet feels... clean.

And then the guilt creeps in.

"What Kind of Person Feels Better?"
You ask yourself this.
If I loved him, why does this feel easier?
If the relationship mattered, why does my body feel lighter?
If I wasn't miserable, why does this feel like air?

Because love and exhaustion can coexist.

Because attachment and depletion can overlap.

Because you can care deeply about someone and still be slowly drained by them.

The guilt comes from the belief that suffering equals sincerity. It doesn't.

Sometimes the truest sign that you were overextended is how quickly your nervous system stabilizes in their absence.

The Nervous System Reset

The body does not lie.

You sleep differently. Maybe not perfectly. But differently.

You are not listening for the garage door. Not bracing for a mood. Not replaying an argument in anticipation of the next one.

Your jaw unclenches. Your stomach settles.

You are not waiting. And waiting is what you had been doing for years. Waiting for him to grow. Waiting for him to understand. Waiting for him to show up consistently. Waiting for tension to pass.

Now there is nothing to wait for. And the stillness is almost shocking.

The Phantom Habit

On that first quiet night, you may still reach for him. Not physically. Habitually.

You think, "I should tell him about that."
"I wonder how his day was."
"He'd like this show."

Then you remember.

You don't have to. There is no one to update. No one to check in with. No one to reassure.

You realize how much of your mental space was occupied by relational maintenance.

You were never alone, even when you were alone.

Now you are alone.

And it feels… spacious.

The Unmonitored Self

Perhaps the most radical shift is this: You are not being watched. Not criticized. Not subtly evaluated. Not responded to with micro-expressions you learned to decode.

You can exist without interpretation. You can wear what you want in your own house. Sit how you want. Cry without someone asking why. Laugh without wondering if you're too loud.

You forgot what it felt like to move without adjustment. To exist without managing perception.

The absence of emotional monitoring is not dramatic. It is gentle. And that gentleness is revolutionary.

The Grief That Follows

Relief does not erase grief. It complicates it.

You may cry that first night. But you are not crying for chaos.

You are crying for: What you hoped it would be. What you invested. What you endured. What you lost. What you almost became.

You are grieving the version of yourself who tried so hard.

You are grieving the fantasy of mutual growth.

You are grieving the future you once pictured.

Grief and relief are not opposites. They are roommates.

The Return of Small Joys

On that first quiet night, something subtle may return.

Curiosity.

You wander around your own space and notice it. You rearrange a lamp. You open a book. You journal without censoring your thoughts. You make tea at midnight. You sit in silence without bracing.

There is no commentary. No undercurrent. No emotional static. No watching what he wants to watch.

Just you and your own interior world.

You remember you have one.

The Guilt Is Conditioning

Let us name the guilt clearly.

You were taught that a woman leaving a relationship should feel loss, not relief. You were taught that endurance is virtuous. That staying proves depth. That working harder proves love.

So if you feel lighter, your mind searches for moral failure.

But relief is not cruelty. It is data. It tells you something was heavy.

And heaviness is not always visible until it lifts.

The Recalibration of Loneliness

Here is a truth most women discover but rarely say out loud: *Loneliness inside a relationship is heavier than solitude outside one.*

In a relationship where you were unseen, you felt alone anyway. You just had to perform companionship on top of it.

Now, at least, the loneliness is honest. It is clean. It is not layered with disappointment.

And honesty is easier to carry.

The First Night You Don't Check

There will be a moment that first night — or the next — when you realize you haven't checked his mood in hours. You haven't wondered if he's upset. You haven't crafted a text to smooth something over. You haven't replayed a conversation. You haven't rehearsed an apology.

And when you notice that absence, you feel the magnitude of what you were doing daily.

You were managing an emotional climate. Now you are simply living in your own.

Reclaiming Interior Space

Interior space is not just physical. It is mental. Emotional. Spiritual.

You begin to hear your own thoughts without interference.

Not the edited version. The unfiltered one.

You may feel anger you suppressed. You may feel sadness you minimized. You may feel ambition you postponed. You may feel desire that had nowhere to go.

Without emotional monitoring, your inner voice grows louder.

At first it is disorienting. Then it becomes grounding.

The Myth of Immediate Regret

You may expect to wake up the next morning panicked. Desperate to call him. Overwhelmed by doubt.

That may happen. Or it may not. And if it doesn't, you may judge yourself again.

But here is what many women discover: The dread they felt before leaving was often about *confrontation*. Not about separation.

Once the confrontation is over, the fear dissolves.

And what remains is quiet.

The Quiet as Teacher

That first quiet night alone is not just an ending. It is an introduction. To yourself. Without mediation. Without distortion. Without adaptation.

You may not know who you are yet. But you will feel something unmistakable: You are not disappearing anymore. You are not shrinking. You are not bracing. You are not adjusting your volume.

You are simply... here.

And here is not lonely.

Here is sovereign.

The Long Game

Do not romanticize this night too quickly.

There will be harder ones. There will be nights when memory feels sharp. When nostalgia edits out the pain. When you miss the familiar weight of his presence.

But that first quiet night is evidence.

Evidence that your nervous system knows the difference between love and labor. Between companionship and management. Between intimacy and vigilance.

You cannot unknow that.

Closing

On the first quiet night alone, you may sit in the dark and feel both ache and ease.

Let both exist. Do not rush to fill the space. Do not numb the relief. Do not punish yourself for breathing easier.

That breath is not betrayal. It is restoration. And restoration is not selfish. It is survival.

Peace does not arrive like fireworks.

It arrives like this: A still room. A steady heartbeat. No one to monitor. No one to manage. No one to shrink for.

Just you. Whole. Unwatched. Unburdened.

And finally — at rest.

Chapter 18

The Backlash

- Male anger at female indifference.

- Social shaming.

- The smear campaign.

There is a moment that often surprises women who leave.

They expect sadness. They expect relief. They expect uncertainty.

What they do not always expect is hostility.

Not always from the partner they left. Sometimes from friends. Sometimes from acquaintances. Sometimes from strangers who feel curiously entitled to an opinion about her decision.

The hostility arrives in different forms. Dismissive laughter. Passive-aggressive comments. Sudden character assessments from people who never previously seemed interested in her character.

The shift can feel bewildering. Because the woman who leaves is rarely staging a revolution. She is not marching through the streets with a banner declaring independence from men.

In most cases, she is simply choosing peace. But that quiet choice can provoke a surprisingly loud reaction.

This is the backlash.

And to understand it, we need to examine something uncomfortable: indifference.

The Most Threatening Emotion

People assume that anger is what destabilizes relationships.

In reality, anger still implies engagement.

The emotion that truly destabilizes power dynamics is *indifference*.

When a woman is angry, she is still invested. She is still negotiating. Still arguing. Still trying to repair.

But when she becomes indifferent, something fundamental changes. She stops trying to convince. She stops chasing resolution. She stops orbiting the emotional gravity of the relationship.

Indifference is not cruelty.

It is simply the absence of emotional dependency.

But to someone who has benefited from that dependency, indifference can feel like an existential threat.

Because if she no longer needs the relationship to feel complete, the relationship must now stand on its own merits. And that is a much harsher test.

Male Anger at Female Indifference

There is a peculiar kind of anger that appears when a woman stops reacting.

It is not the anger of betrayal. It is the anger of lost leverage.

For years, the emotional dynamic may have been predictable. She expressed concerns. He minimized them. She pushed harder. He withdrew. Round and round.

But when she disengages — when she stops arguing, stops persuading, stops trying to manage his responses — the familiar dance collapses. And in the absence of that dance, frustration appears.

Because anger, in this context, is often an attempt to restore the old dynamic.

If she becomes upset, she is back in the arena. If she defends herself, she is participating again. If she argues, the relationship is still emotionally alive.

Indifference removes the stage.

And some people experience that removal as an insult.

The Fragility of the Narrative

Many men grow up with a particular narrative about themselves.

They are the center of the relationship. The decision-maker. The one whose approval matters most.

This narrative is not always consciously held, but it often shapes expectations.

A woman's dissatisfaction can be tolerated. Her frustration can be managed.

But her indifference disrupts the story entirely. Because indifference suggests something far more destabilizing than anger.

It suggests that the relationship may not have been essential to her identity after all.

And if the relationship was not essential, what does that say about the role he believed he was playing?

The backlash often emerges from this disorientation.

The story he told himself about the relationship no longer matches reality.

Someone must be blamed for that discrepancy. And the easiest target is the woman who left.

The Language of Backlash

Backlash has its own vocabulary.

It rarely sounds like pure rage. It usually arrives disguised as critique.

She's selfish. She's cold. She's unrealistic. She expects too much.

The accusations share a common theme.

The problem is not the relationship. The problem is the woman's expectations.

If she had simply lowered them, the narrative suggests, everything would have been fine.

This rhetorical move is clever because it avoids examining the original imbalance.

Instead of asking whether the relationship was equitable, the conversation becomes a referendum on the woman's character. Was she patient enough? Supportive enough? Forgiving enough?

The structure remains unexamined.

Only the woman is scrutinized.

Social Shaming

Backlash is not limited to the former partner.

Communities often participate.

Friends who once expressed sympathy may begin offering unsolicited advice. Family members may frame the departure as a mistake. Coworkers may deliver subtle comments about the difficulty of "finding someone these days."

The tone is rarely openly hostile. Instead, it carries a faint note of condescension.

Are you sure you didn't overreact?

Relationships take work.

Nobody's perfect.

These phrases sound reasonable.

But their cumulative effect is pressure. Pressure to reconsider. Pressure to soften the narrative. Pressure to accept that leaving might have been impulsive.

The woman is gently encouraged to reinterpret her own experience.

The Comfort of the Status Quo

Why do people participate in this shaming? Often because the alternative is unsettling.

If a woman can walk away from a long-term relationship simply because it no longer serves her well-being, the implications ripple outward.

Other people must then examine their own relationships. Are *they* happy? Or merely accustomed?

Questioning these things is uncomfortable.

So it is easier to conclude that the woman who left must be unreasonable.

Her departure becomes an anomaly rather than a possibility. And the status quo remains intact.

The Smear Campaign

In some cases, backlash escalates.

What begins as criticism becomes character assassination. Stories circulate. Selective memories emerge. Private disagreements are reframed as evidence of instability.

The woman who left becomes the villain of a narrative she did not write.

Smear campaigns serve a very specific psychological function. They restore coherence.

If the relationship ended because the woman was unreasonable, selfish, or disloyal, then the partner who was left behind does not need to examine his own behavior.

The story becomes tidy again. And tidy stories are emotionally convenient.

Unfortunately, they are rarely accurate.

Reputation as Control

Smear campaigns rely on a powerful social currency: reputation.

Humans are deeply sensitive to how they are perceived by others. Threatening a person's reputation can therefore function as a form of control.

If a woman fears being labeled difficult, she may hesitate to assert her needs. If she fears being labeled cold, she may continue providing emotional labor. If she fears being labeled bitter, she may soften the truth about why she left.

The smear campaign leverages these fears. It sends a message not only to the woman who left but also to other women who might be watching.

Leave, and this could happen to you.

The Gendered Double Standard

Men who leave relationships are rarely subjected to the same level of scrutiny.

They may be described as restless. Or searching. Or simply moving on.

Women who leave, however, are often asked to justify their decision repeatedly.

Did he cheat? Was there abuse?

If the answer is no, the implication is that leaving may have been excessive.

This standard reveals a deeper assumption: A woman must have a dramatic reason to exit a relationship.

Discomfort is insufficient. Unequal emotional labor is insufficient. Chronic dissatisfaction is insufficient.

She must produce evidence of wrongdoing before her departure is considered legitimate.

Otherwise, the narrative of selfishness returns.

The Cost of Noncompliance

Backlash functions as a warning.

It reminds women that stepping outside the expected script carries consequences. Social approval may be withdrawn. Reputation may be challenged. Support networks may shift.

These consequences can feel intimidating, especially during the early stages of independence.

But they also reveal something important. If the cost of leaving includes criticism and gossip, it suggests that staying was never entirely voluntary.

Social pressure was part of the equation.

And recognizing that pressure can be liberating. Because once you see it clearly, it becomes easier to resist.

The Strength of Indifference

Ironically, the very quality that provokes backlash — indifference — also provides protection.

When a woman stops seeking validation from the people criticizing her, their words lose much of their force.

This does not happen overnight. Years of conditioning cannot be erased instantly.

But gradually, something shifts. The opinions that once felt decisive begin to feel optional. The narratives that once felt threatening begin to feel predictable.

And the backlash, once overwhelming, begins to look strangely repetitive. Almost scripted.

A Familiar Pattern

Women who share their experiences often discover that the backlash they faced was not unique.

The same accusations appear again and again. Selfish. Cold. Difficult. Unrealistic.

These labels function like stamps applied to any woman who refuses to perform the expected role.

Once you recognize the pattern, the accusations lose some of their sting. They are not personal insights. They are cultural reflexes.

The Backlash as Confirmation

There is an unexpected way to interpret backlash.

Not as proof that the woman made a mistake. But as confirmation that the decision disrupted a system that relied on her compliance.

If leaving provokes anger, gossip, or attempts to undermine her credibility, it suggests that her presence once served a function.

She was stabilizing something. She was absorbing something. She was maintaining a balance that others had grown accustomed to.

When that function disappears, the system reacts.

And reaction is a form of acknowledgment.

The Quiet After the Storm

Backlash rarely lasts forever.

People eventually find new topics to discuss. Like the headlines, new stories capture their attention.

The woman who left becomes less interesting as her life moves forward.

What remains is something quieter. Space.

The space to rebuild identity without constant negotiation. The space to cultivate relationships that do not require performance. The space to rediscover preferences that were once buried beneath compromise. In this space, the accusations that once felt urgent begin to fade.

Because they were never the central story. They were merely the noise surrounding a transition.

Reclaiming the Narrative

One of the most powerful steps a woman can take after leaving is to reclaim the narrative of her own life.

Not defensively. Not combatively. Simply honestly.

She does not need to persuade everyone. She does not need universal approval.

She only needs clarity.

Clarity about why she left. Clarity about what she values. Clarity about the kind of life she intends to build.

When that clarity is present, the backlash loses its ability to destabilize. It becomes background static.

The Final Realization

The backlash is often framed as evidence that leaving was disruptive.

But disruption is not always negative.

Sometimes disruption is the necessary consequence of refusing to continue a pattern that was quietly draining you.

If a system depends on your silence, your emotional labor, or your willingness to tolerate imbalance, your departure will always seem radical.

Not because it is inherently extreme. But because the system never expected you to leave.

And that is precisely why the backlash appears.

Not to punish the woman who left. But to remind the others still watching that leaving is possible.

Once that possibility becomes visible, it spreads. Quietly. One life at a time.

I was the first mother in my teenage son's peer group to leave my husband. Together for 19 years, married and quietly desperate for 15 of them. A few months later, my son announced that the mother of one of his peers had done the same.

"Mom, what have your started?" he asked jokingly.

"A quiet revolution, it seems" was my reply.

Chapter 19

Practical Separation

- Financial disentanglement.

- Housing.

- Boundaries.

Leaving, in theory, is emotional.

Leaving, in reality, is logistical.

The decision itself — the moment a woman finally admits to herself that she wants out — can feel like a lightning strike. Clarity arrives. The fog lifts. The truth becomes undeniable.

But after the emotional shift comes something far less cinematic. Paperwork. Accounts. Keys. Addresses. Furniture. Phone plans. Insurance policies. Streaming passwords.

All the quiet infrastructure of shared life.

Romantic narratives tend to treat separation as a dramatic turning point. One argument, one declaration, one decisive departure.

In truth, separation is rarely a single event. It is a process.

And like any process involving two lives that have been intertwined — financially, spatially, socially — it requires deliberate untangling.

This chapter is not about heartbreak. It is about the mechanics of leaving.

Because independence is not built on courage alone. It is built on systems.

The Myth of the Clean Break

Popular culture loves the idea of the clean break. A suitcase. A slammed door. A new apartment. A woman standing alone on a balcony, wind in her hair, liberated.

Sometimes reality does resemble this. But more often, separation looks messier.

It involves shared leases. Shared mortgages. Shared bank accounts. Shared pets.

Years of life woven together cannot be instantly undone.

This reality is one of the reasons many women delay leaving relationships long after they recognize the emotional cost.

The logistical barrier feels overwhelming. Where will I live? How will I afford it? What will happen to our things? Who gets to keep the dog?

These questions are not trivial. They are practical concerns that deserve thoughtful answers.

But they are also solvable problems.

And once women begin approaching separation as a logistical project rather than an emotional catastrophe, something shifts.

The exit becomes manageable.

Financial Disentanglement

Money is often the most intimidating part of separation.

For generations, financial dependence kept women trapped in relationships long after the emotional connection had deteriorated.

Even today, when many women earn their own income, finances remain intertwined in ways that can complicate departure.

Shared bank accounts. Joint credit cards. Mortgages. Car loans. Insurance policies. Subscriptions. Debt.

The first step in financial disentanglement is simple but powerful: visibility. You cannot separate what you cannot see.

So the work begins with information. What accounts exist? Whose name is on them? What debts are shared? What assets are jointly owned?

Many women discover, sometimes to their surprise, that they have not been fully aware of the financial architecture of their own household.

This is not a personal failure. It is the result of a long cultural tradition in which men often managed financial systems while women managed emotional ones.

Separation reverses that dynamic. Now the systems must be examined. Carefully. Methodically. Without panic.

Creating Financial Independence

Once visibility exists, independence can begin.

Separate bank accounts. Separate credit lines. Separate financial plans.

This transition does not always happen overnight. Sometimes it unfolds gradually, especially if the couple shares large financial obligations.

But even small steps matter. Opening an individual account. Redirecting income. Building a private emergency fund.

These actions may seem modest, but they create psychological shifts.

Money represents security. And security changes the emotional landscape of leaving.

When a woman knows she can support herself, the decision to separate becomes less frightening. The unknown shrinks. The future becomes navigable.

The Emotional Weight of Money

Financial disentanglement is not purely practical.

Money carries emotional symbolism. Who paid for what. Who sacrificed career opportunities. Who contributed more. Whose parents helped with the home loan?

These narratives can become battlegrounds during separation.

It is tempting to revisit every financial decision made during the relationship. To assign credit. To assign blame.

But this rarely leads to clarity. Instead, it prolongs conflict.

Practical separation requires a different approach. Not moral accounting. Just logistical resolution.

What exists. What needs to be divided. What must be closed.

The goal is not perfect fairness — which is often impossible to achieve — but functional independence.

Housing: Reclaiming Physical Space

Housing is often the most visible symbol of separation.

Where will she live? This question carries both practical and emotional weight.

The home is rarely just a building. It is the container of shared history. Furniture chosen together. Walls that have witnessed arguments and celebrations. Rooms filled with memories.

Leaving that space can feel like abandoning a chapter of life.

Staying in it alone can feel equally strange.

Some women move immediately. Others remain temporarily while practical arrangements unfold.

There is no universal right choice. But the key principle remains the same: the living space must support the life that comes next. Not the life that just ended.

The Power of a Room of One's Own

For many women, living alone after a long relationship brings an unexpected sensation.

Silence. Not the tense silence that follows an argument. But genuine quiet.

No footsteps in the next room. No emotional temperature to monitor.

No subtle awareness of another person's mood.

At first, this silence can feel unfamiliar.

Humans are adaptable creatures, and when we spend years sharing space, our nervous systems adjust to constant companionship.

But gradually, the quiet becomes restorative. The home transforms from a negotiation space into a sanctuary. A place where every object, every schedule, every decision belongs to the woman herself.

This transformation is more powerful than it might appear.

Because physical space shapes psychological experience. A room of one's own is not merely symbolic. It is stabilizing.

Rebuilding a Home

Creating a new living environment after separation can be both daunting and exhilarating.

Practical considerations appear first. Rent or mortgage payments. Utilities. Location. Proximity to work and community.

But once those basics are established, something interesting happens.

The home becomes a canvas.

For years, the living space may have been a compromise between two sets of preferences.

Now it becomes an expression of one. The colors on the walls. The arrangement of furniture. The music playing in the background.

Small choices begin to accumulate. And with each choice, identity reasserts itself.

This is not about decorating. It is about reclaiming agency.

Boundaries

Perhaps the most important element of practical separation is boundaries.

Separation does not automatically dissolve emotional habits.

If a woman spent years managing her partner's moods, that instinct may continue even after the relationship ends. He calls, frustrated. She feels compelled to soothe. He asks for help with a problem. She instinctively steps in.

These patterns are deeply ingrained.

Boundaries interrupt them.

They create distance where constant availability once existed. This does not require hostility. It requires clarity.

The First Boundary: Communication

Communication is often the first area where boundaries must be established.

How often will they speak? About what topics? Through which channels?

These questions may feel awkward, but they are necessary.

Without boundaries, the emotional dynamic of the relationship can persist long after the official separation. Late-night conversations. Emotional check-ins. Requests for advice.

These interactions blur the line between past and present.

Boundaries clarify the transition. They signal that the relationship, as it once existed, is over.

Emotional Boundaries

Emotional boundaries can be even more challenging.

Former partners may continue seeking reassurance, validation, or sympathy.

After all, the woman may have filled that role for years.

But separation means relinquishing that responsibility. He is now responsible for managing his own emotional landscape.

This shift can provoke resistance. Accusations of coldness. Claims that she has changed.

In truth, she has. She is no longer functioning as his emotional regulator. And that is precisely what separation requires.

The Temptation to Soften

Women are often socialized to soften boundaries. To cushion them with explanations. To apologize for them.

"I'm sorry, but I just need some space."

While politeness is admirable, excessive softening can undermine the boundary itself.

A boundary is not a request. It is a statement.
"I will not be available for this conversation."
"I will not discuss that topic."
"I will not continue this pattern."

Clarity may feel uncomfortable at first.

But ambiguity invites negotiation. And separation requires firmness.

The Role of Community

Practical separation becomes easier when women do not attempt it alone.

Friends. Family. Professional advisors. Support networks provide both logistical assistance and emotional stability.

Someone may help with moving. Someone may offer temporary housing. Someone may simply listen without judgment.

Community acts as scaffolding during the transition. And in many cases, women discover that the relationships surrounding them are stronger than they realized.

Because once the central partnership dissolves, other connections have space to expand.

The Unexpected Relief

Amid all the logistics — the bank accounts, the housing searches, the boundary conversations — many women notice something surprising.

Relief.

Not constant joy. Not immediate confidence. But relief.

The relief of not having to monitor someone else's moods. The relief of not having to negotiate every decision. The relief of knowing that the emotional labor that once consumed so much energy is no longer required.

This relief can coexist with sadness.

Relationships rarely end without grief. But grief and relief are not opposites. They are companions.

A New Structure

Practical separation ultimately creates a new structure for life.

New routines. New financial systems. New living spaces. New emotional boundaries.

These structures may feel fragile at first. Like scaffolding around a building still under construction.

But over time, they solidify. The systems that once supported a shared life are replaced by systems that support an individual one.

And within those systems, something quietly powerful emerges: Autonomy.

The ability to make decisions without negotiation. The ability to spend time without explanation. The ability to build a life that reflects personal priorities rather than shared compromises.

The Quiet Triumph

Separation rarely produces a single triumphant moment. There is no universal day when a woman suddenly declares herself completely free.

Instead, the triumph appears in small moments. The first evening in a new home. The first paycheck deposited into an individual account. The first boundary held without apology.

These moments accumulate. And with each one, independence becomes less theoretical. It becomes lived reality.

Practical separation, in the end, is not merely about leaving a relationship.

It is about constructing a life where staying is never again required by circumstance. Only by choice.

And that distinction changes everything.

Chapter 20

Surviving the Doubt

- Nights when conditioning resurfaces.

- How to resist returning out of fear.

There is a moment after the logistics are handled.

The accounts have been separated. The boxes unpacked. The new routines quietly established.

From the outside, the separation appears complete.

But internally, another stage begins: Doubt.

Not the dramatic doubt of crisis — the quieter kind. The kind that appears late at night when the house is silent and the mind begins replaying old conversations.

Did I overreact? Was it really that bad? Maybe I should have tried harder.

These thoughts do not arrive because the woman suddenly wants the life she left behind.

They arrive because conditioning does not evaporate overnight.
Leaving a relationship may take courage.

But unlearning the narratives that kept you there takes time.

The Echo of Old Scripts

Most women who leave long-term relationships are surprised by how persistent the old scripts can be.

Even after months of independence, certain phrases echo in the mind.
Relationships take work.
Nobody's perfect.
You'll regret this.
You're expecting too much.

These messages have been repeated so often — by family, friends, culture — that they become internal voices.

The mind, seeking stability, tries to restore familiar frameworks.

And the familiar framework says something simple: Partnership equals success.

So when the partnership ends, the brain interprets the change as failure — even if the lived experience of the relationship told a very different story.

This is not weakness. It is conditioning.

The Nights When Doubt Returns

Doubt tends to arrive at night.

During the day, life is active. Work demands attention. Friends provide conversation. Errands fill time.

But at night, the nervous system slows. The quiet expands. And the mind begins to wander.

This is when the old questions surface. Not because they are accurate. But because the brain is wired to revisit unresolved experiences.

Loneliness can amplify the effect.

Even women who feel deeply relieved after leaving sometimes encounter moments of loneliness.

Humans are social creatures. We are designed to seek connection. And when connection is absent in the familiar form of partnership, the mind begins scanning the past.

Perhaps it wasn't so bad. Perhaps I was too harsh. Perhaps I should go back.

These thoughts can feel persuasive in the darkness.

But morning often reveals them differently.

The Distortion of Nostalgia

One of the most powerful psychological forces during this stage is nostalgia.

Nostalgia edits. It removes the exhausting parts of the relationship and preserves the warm ones.

The mind replays small moments. A shared joke. A holiday trip. A quiet evening on the couch.

These memories are real. But they are incomplete.

They omit the context that led to separation. The abuse of trust. The repeated arguments. The emotional labor. The feeling of walking on eggshells.

Nostalgia is not lying. But it is selective.

And selective memory can create the illusion that the relationship was better than it actually felt while you were living inside it.

The Conditioning of Female Responsibility

Another source of doubt comes from the deeply embedded belief that women are responsible for maintaining relationships.

When a relationship ends, many women instinctively ask: What did I do wrong?

Even when the reasons for leaving were clear. Even when the imbalance was obvious.

Women are trained to evaluate their own performance first. Did I communicate clearly enough? Did I give him enough chances? Did I support him properly?

These questions can be useful when they lead to growth.

But they can also become traps when they obscure a more fundamental truth: Relationships require mutual effort.

No amount of communication can repair a dynamic where one person refuses to participate.

The Fear of the Unknown

Doubt is not always about the past.

Often it is about the future.

Humans prefer certainty, even imperfect certainty, to uncertainty.

A relationship, even an unsatisfying one, provides a kind of structure. There is someone to call. Someone to share meals with. Someone to occupy the space beside you.

When that structure disappears, the future feels less predictable. What if I never meet anyone again? What if I *do* grow old alone? What if I made a mistake?

These fears are understandable.

But they are often exaggerated by cultural narratives that portray partnership as the only path to stability.

In reality, stability can come from many sources. Friendship. Community. Work. Creative pursuits. Self-trust.

But those forms of stability can take time to develop.

And during the transition, the mind may gravitate toward the familiar.

The Urge to Return

For some women, doubt evolves into temptation. Not because the relationship has suddenly improved. But because returning seems easier than continuing forward.

Going back promises immediate relief from uncertainty.

The familiar routines resume. The social questions stop. The identity of "partner" returns.

But this relief is often temporary. Because the original dynamics rarely disappear.

If the relationship required constant emotional labor before, it will likely require it again.

If boundaries were ignored before, they will likely be tested again.

Returning without fundamental change simply reinstates the old system.

And the reasons for leaving eventually reappear.

Fear vs. Clarity

One of the most useful distinctions during this stage is the difference between fear and clarity.

Fear asks: What if I *do* end up alone? What if I regret this? What if I can't handle independence?

Clarity asks a different question: Was the life I was living sustainable?

Fear focuses on hypothetical futures.

Clarity remembers lived reality.

During moments of doubt, it can be helpful to return to that reality.
What did daily life actually feel like?
What patterns kept repeating?
What needs remained unmet?

These questions anchor the mind in experience rather than speculation.

Rebuilding Self-Trust

Perhaps the most important task during this stage is rebuilding self-trust.

Leaving a relationship requires believing your own perception.

Believing that your experience matters. Believing that your desire for peace is legitimate.

But doubt can erode that belief.

The mind begins second-guessing itself. Maybe I misunderstood. Maybe I exaggerated.

Rebuilding self-trust involves honoring the decision you made. Not blindly. But respectfully.

You made that decision for a reason.

You examined your life and concluded that something needed to change.

That process deserves recognition. Even if uncertainty remains.

The Role of Memory

One practical strategy many women find helpful is writing down the reasons they left.

Not as a document for others. But as a reminder for themselves.

During moments of nostalgia, the mind tends to highlight the pleasant memories.

A written record can restore balance. It can remind you of the patterns that led to separation.

The arguments that never resolved. The exhaustion that accumulated.

This is not about dwelling on negativity. It is about preserving accuracy.

Memory alone can become distorted. Documentation provides perspective.

Learning to Sit With Uncertainty

A central challenge of this stage is learning to tolerate uncertainty.

The future is not fully mapped. There may not be an immediate replacement for the relationship that ended. But uncertainty is not inherently dangerous.

In fact, it is often the space where new possibilities emerge.

Many women who leave long-term relationships eventually build lives that feel more expansive than they imagined. New friendships. New creative pursuits. New forms of intimacy.

But these possibilities rarely appear instantly. They develop gradually.

And during the early stages, uncertainty is simply part of the terrain.

The Myth of Immediate Happiness

Another source of doubt comes from unrealistic expectations about life after separation.

Some cultural narratives portray leaving as a gateway to instant liberation.

A woman exits a relationship and immediately flourishes.

Reality is usually more complex. There may be loneliness. Moments of grief. Periods of adjustment.

This does not mean the decision was wrong. It simply means that transitions take time.

Freedom is not always euphoric in the beginning. Sometimes it feels quiet. Sometimes it feels uncertain.

But quiet and uncertain can still be healthier than constant emotional strain.

The Strength of Staying Gone

Resisting the urge to return requires patience.

Not heroic willpower. Just patience.

The mind needs time to recalibrate. New routines need time to stabilize. Identity needs time to evolve.

What feels uncomfortable today may feel normal six months from now.

What feels lonely tonight may feel peaceful next year.

The key is allowing the transition to unfold without rushing to erase discomfort.

When the Doubt Passes

Something interesting happens if a woman allows the doubt to run its course without acting on it.

Gradually, the intensity fades. The questions become less urgent. The nights become quieter. The mind begins focusing more on the present than the past.

This shift is subtle. There is no dramatic moment when doubt disappears entirely.

But the emotional center of gravity moves.

Instead of constantly revisiting the relationship that ended, attention begins moving forward. Toward the life that is still being built.

A New Relationship With Yourself

Surviving the doubt ultimately creates something unexpected.

A new relationship.

Not with another person. With yourself.

For perhaps the first time in years, your decisions are guided primarily by your own internal compass.

Not by the need to maintain harmony with a partner. Not by the pressure to preserve a relationship at any cost.

Just by your understanding of what makes your life feel stable, meaningful, and peaceful.

This relationship with yourself becomes the foundation for everything that follows.

Future partnerships, if they appear, will be evaluated differently. Friendships will deepen. Priorities will clarify.

But none of that requires rushing. For now, surviving the doubt is enough.

Because doubt is not a sign that the decision to leave was wrong.

It is simply the mind adjusting to a new reality. And adjustment takes time.

The important thing is that the life you left behind no longer defines the life ahead.

Even on the nights when the old scripts whisper otherwise.

Chapter 21

Owning the Narrative

- You did not fail.

- You chose peace.

- That is power.

There is a moment that arrives after the doubt quiets.

It does not come with fireworks. It does not announce itself dramatically.

It arrives slowly, almost shyly.

One morning you wake up and realize something small but profound: You are no longer explaining yourself. Not to friends. Not to strangers. Not even to the voice in your own head.

The story has changed.

For a long time, the story sounded like this: The relationship ended. It didn't work out. Maybe I failed.

But eventually something shifts.

The words rearrange themselves. I chose to leave. I chose something better for myself. I chose peace.

And suddenly the entire meaning of the past transforms.

Because the narrative was never about failure. It was about freedom.

The Power of the Story We Tell

Human beings live inside stories. Not just the stories in books or films, but the stories we construct about our own lives.

These narratives shape how we interpret events.

They determine whether we see ourselves as victims, survivors, failures, or architects of change.

When a relationship ends, the cultural script offers only a few interpretations. A breakup is tragic. A divorce is unfortunate. A woman alone is somehow incomplete.

The assumption embedded in these interpretations is simple: The goal was partnership.

If partnership ended, the goal was not achieved. Therefore, the outcome must be failure.

This logic is rarely examined. But it quietly governs how women interpret their own lives.

The Cultural Definition of Success

For generations, female success was defined relationally.

A successful woman was one who secured a partner. Preferably early. Preferably permanently.

Marriage was treated as a destination. Once reached, the journey was considered complete.

Everything else — career, creativity, travel, intellectual life — was secondary.

If a woman reached adulthood without securing a partner, the culture assumed something had gone wrong.

Maybe she was too ambitious. Too picky. Too intimidating. Too independent.

The language varied, but the implication remained constant: A woman without a partner had deviated from the expected path.

When the Story Collapses

But what happens when the expected path stops making sense?

What happens when the partnership itself becomes the source of exhaustion rather than fulfillment?

For many women, this realization emerges gradually.

At first it feels like confusion. Why am I so tired? Why does this relationship require so much effort? *Why does peace feel easier when he isn't here?*

These questions challenge the narrative that partnership automatically improves life.

And when the questions accumulate, the old story begins to crack. Because if the relationship is not delivering stability, support, or joy, then the premise of the narrative becomes questionable.

Maybe partnership is not the goal. Maybe the goal is something else.

Peace as a Radical Metric

What if success were measured differently?

What if the central question were not: Did you secure a partner?

But instead: Is your life peaceful?

Peace is rarely used as a metric for success. Yet it may be one of the most reliable indicators of well-being.

Peace means the nervous system can relax. Peace means your home feels safe. Peace means you do not wake up anticipating emotional turbulence.

Peace does not require perfection. It simply requires stability.

When a woman leaves a relationship that disrupted that stability, she is not abandoning success.

She is redefining it.

The Courage of Refusal

Leaving a relationship requires confronting multiple layers of pressure.

There is the internal pressure of doubt. But there is also external pressure.

Family members may question the decision. Friends may worry. Colleagues may speculate. Even strangers feel entitled to commentary.
"You're giving up."
"Every relationship has problems."
"You'll regret this later."

These statements are not always malicious. Often they reflect genuine concern.

But they also reveal how deeply the cultural narrative is embedded.

Partnership is assumed to be the correct outcome. Anything that disrupts that outcome must be reconsidered.

Choosing to leave means refusing that narrative. And refusal is uncomfortable for people who depend on the narrative remaining intact.

The Myth of Endurance
One of the most powerful cultural myths about relationships is the idea that endurance equals virtue.

Women are praised for patience. Admired for loyalty. Celebrated for sticking it out through difficulty.

But endurance is not always noble.

Sometimes endurance is simply prolonged discomfort.

Staying in a relationship that erodes your sense of self does not transform suffering into virtue. It merely extends the suffering.

Yet the cultural story often rewards endurance and punishes departure.

A woman who leaves may be labeled impatient. Selfish. Unrealistic.

But these labels lose their power once the narrative changes.

Because the question is no longer: Did she endure long enough?

The question becomes: Did she protect her own well-being?

The Reframing of Failure

Failure implies an objective standard.

To fail an exam means you did not achieve the required score. To fail a business venture means the enterprise collapsed.

But relationships are not standardized tests. They are dynamic interactions between two people.

When a relationship ends, it is not necessarily evidence that someone failed.

Sometimes it is evidence that two individuals were incompatible. Sometimes it is evidence that one person was unwilling to grow. Sometimes it is evidence that the conditions required for mutual flourishing were simply not present.

In these cases, ending the relationship is not failure. It is recognition.

Recognition that continuing would not improve the situation. Recognition that peace matters more than preserving appearances.

The Liberation of Self-Definition

When a woman steps outside the traditional narrative of partnership, something unexpected happens.

She becomes the author of her own definition of success.

Instead of inheriting expectations, she creates them.

Success might mean building a career that feels meaningful. It might mean cultivating deep friendships. It might mean traveling, studying, creating, or mentoring. It might mean simply living a quiet life free from emotional turbulence.

The possibilities expand because they are no longer constrained by a single relational milestone.

The absence of partnership does not create emptiness. It creates space.

The Reactions of Others

When a woman redefines her narrative, the reactions around her can be revealing.

Some people respond with admiration. Others respond with confusion. And some respond with discomfort.

This discomfort often arises because her decision challenges assumptions they have built their own lives around.

If partnership is supposed to guarantee happiness, then a woman who leaves a partnership in pursuit of peace disrupts that belief.

It introduces a possibility that many people would rather avoid considering.

That possibility is simple: Staying may not always be the better choice.

But her decision is not a referendum on anyone else's life. It is simply a reflection of her own experience.

And once she recognizes that, the reactions of others become less significant.

The Quiet Confidence That Follows

Owning your narrative does not require loud declarations. It does not require convincing anyone.

It simply requires living consistently with your own understanding of what makes life sustainable.

Over time, this consistency produces a quiet confidence. Not arrogance. Not defiance. Just steadiness.

The questions from others lose their urgency. The need to justify your choices disappears.

Because the narrative has stabilized internally.

You know why you made the decision you made. And that knowledge becomes enough.

The Return of Possibility

One of the most surprising outcomes of leaving an unsatisfying relationship is the return of possibility.

When emotional energy is no longer consumed by constant negotiation, something opens.

Time expands. Attention becomes available again. Interests that were neglected begin to resurface.

Some women rediscover creative pursuits they abandoned years earlier. Others invest more deeply in friendships. Some simply enjoy the luxury of uninterrupted solitude.

The life that emerges is not necessarily dramatic.

But it is authentic. And authenticity has a stability that performative happiness rarely achieves.

The Difference Between Loneliness and Solitude

The cultural narrative often conflates being alone with being lonely.

But these are not the same experience.

Loneliness is the feeling of being disconnected from meaningful connection.

Solitude is the experience of being alone without distress.

Many women discover that solitude can be deeply nourishing. It allows the mind to rest. It creates space for reflection. It removes the constant negotiation required in relationships that lack balance.

This does not mean a woman will never experience loneliness. Everyone does at times.

But loneliness is not solved simply by being partnered.

And solitude is not inherently a problem that needs solving.

The Power of Peace

Peace is often underestimated. It does not produce dramatic stories. It does not attract attention.

But it provides something more valuable than excitement. It provides sustainability.

A peaceful life allows creativity to flourish. It allows friendships to deepen. It allows the body and mind to recover from chronic stress.

When a woman chooses peace over a relationship that disrupted it, she is not retreating from life.

She is protecting the conditions that allow life to unfold more fully.

The End of the Old Story

At some point, the old narrative loses its grip completely.

The idea that you "failed" at a relationship begins to feel strange.

Because the life you are living now no longer resembles failure. It feels stable. It feels authentic. It feels yours.

And when that realization settles in, the cultural script loses its authority.

The story no longer belongs to the culture. It belongs to *you*.

The Beginning of the Next Chapter

Owning your narrative does not mean rejecting the possibility of future relationships.

It simply means those relationships are no longer required to validate your life.

If love appears, it will be evaluated differently. Not as salvation. Not as completion. But as an addition.

A partnership will need to *enhance* the peace that already exists.

Otherwise it will not be worth the cost.

This has been my mantra for years, and I paraphrase Warsan Shire, the Somali English poet, who articulates it perfectly:

"I'll only have you if you're sweeter than my solitude."

This shift changes everything.

Because it transforms relationships from necessities into choices. And choice is power.

The Truth That Remains

So let us state the truth clearly.

You did not fail. You observed your life honestly. You recognized that something essential was missing. And you acted.

You chose a path that preserved your well-being rather than sacrificing it to maintain appearances.

That is not weakness. That is clarity. That is courage. That is power.

Because the real success was never securing a relationship.

The real success is building a life that feels sustainable, meaningful, and peaceful.

And if peace required walking away from a partnership that could not offer it, then the choice was not a failure.

It was a correction.

A correction that returned the story of your life to the person who should have been writing it all along.

You.

And from this point forward, the narrative is yours to define.

PART V: THE PEACE

What "Alone" Actually Looks Like

After the storm of leaving, there is a strange and quiet phase that few people talk about.

It is not dramatic. It is not tragic.

It is simply life — reorganizing itself around your own center.

For years, perhaps decades, your attention may have been oriented outward: toward someone else's moods, someone else's needs, someone else's expectations.

Partnership required constant calibration. Decisions were negotiated. Time was shared. Emotional weather was monitored.

Then suddenly, the atmosphere clears. Not perfectly. Not permanently. But noticeably.

You wake up and realize something subtle has changed: *the day belongs to you.*

There is no emotional barometer to check before speaking. No tension humming in the background of the house. No invisible negotiations about how your time, energy, or body should be used.

At first, this quiet can feel unfamiliar. Even unsettling.

A lifetime of conditioning has taught women that being alone is a deficit — something to fix quickly, something to escape.

But once the noise fades, another reality becomes visible.

Peace.

Not the sterile quiet of isolation, but the spacious calm of a life that is no longer organized around emotional maintenance.

You discover how much energy becomes available when you are not managing someone else's moods.

You notice how your body relaxes when the atmosphere of your home is predictable.

You rediscover interests, friendships, curiosities that had slowly receded behind the demands of partnership.

And something else emerges as well: *sovereignty*.

Not loneliness. Not bitterness.

Sovereignty. The ability to design your life deliberately. To choose what enters it. To decide what stays.

Part V is about this stage — the one the culture rarely depicts honestly.

Not the frightening caricature of the "woman alone." But the lived reality of women who discover that solitude can be expansive, creative, and deeply stabilizing.

This is what "alone" actually looks like.

And once you see it clearly, the old warning — *You'll die alone* — loses its power completely.

Because the truth is far more interesting.

You are not alone.

You are finally free.

Chapter 22

The Architecture of a Peaceful Life

- Rituals.

- Personal sovereignty.

- Designing your days.

Peace is not an accident.

It does not appear automatically once a relationship ends. It is not a prize that materializes simply because you chose independence. Peace, like any durable structure, must be built.

Most women who leave long partnerships discover something quietly astonishing: they have spent years living inside a structure they did not design.

The rhythms of their days were shaped by negotiation. The atmosphere of their home was shaped by someone else's moods. The allocation of their time was shaped by compromise.

This is not inherently wrong. Partnership involves shared space and shared schedules.

But when a relationship ends, a rare opportunity appears.

For the first time in years, perhaps decades, the architecture of your life is yours to design.

And design matters. Because peace is not simply the absence of conflict. Peace is structure that supports calm.

Peace is a life arranged deliberately enough that your nervous system can finally exhale.

The Myth of the Empty Life

One of the most persistent myths about women living alone is that their lives become empty.

The cultural image is almost comically bleak: quiet apartments, silent dinners, evenings spent waiting for something — or someone — to happen.

But when women actually begin building lives around their own priorities, the opposite tends to occur.

The days fill. Not with obligations imposed from outside, but with choices made from within.

Morning routines develop. Friendships deepen. Interests re-emerge.

The calendar begins to reflect something new: *intention.*

When no one else is structuring your life, you must structure it yourself.

And that responsibility, far from being a burden, becomes a form of freedom.

Rituals: The Framework of Calm

One of the first discoveries women often make after leaving a draining relationship is the power of ritual.

Ritual is not about superstition or rigid habit. It is about rhythm.

Small, repeated actions that create stability.

In relationships characterized by emotional volatility, daily life can feel unpredictable. A simple evening can be interrupted by tension. A quiet morning can be disrupted by someone else's stress.

When you live alone, the environment becomes more stable.

And rituals begin to form naturally. Morning coffee in the same chair. A quiet stroll through familiar streets. An evening glass of wine on the porch. Music playing softly while preparing dinner. A relaxing bath bomb and candles.

These rituals may appear trivial from the outside.

But they perform an important psychological function: they tell the body it is safe.

Predictable rhythms calm the nervous system.

After years of emotional vigilance, this calm can feel extraordinary.

The First Sovereign Morning

Many women remember the first morning when the quiet feels fully theirs.

No one else's alarm. No tension in the air. No anticipation of how someone else might be feeling that day.

Just the simple awareness that the morning belongs to you.

This is sovereignty in its most ordinary form.

You decide when to wake. What to eat. How to spend the first hour of the day.

These decisions may seem small. But after years of negotiating daily life with another person, they feel profound.

Because autonomy restores something many women did not realize they had lost: psychological space.

Designing Your Days

Once the immediate aftermath of separation settles, a more interesting question emerges:

How do you want your life to feel?

Not what it should look like to others. Not what cultural expectations prescribe. But how it should feel to inhabit.

Some women design lives filled with social activity — dinners, travel, vibrant circles of friends.

Others design quieter lives — long walks, reading, creative work.

Some pursue ambitious careers. Others prioritize flexibility and calm.

There is no single correct blueprint.

But there is one common principle: intention.

Instead of reacting constantly to another person's needs, you begin choosing how your time is structured.

That shift transforms everyday life.

The Power of a Controlled Environment

A peaceful life is often built on something surprisingly practical: environment.

Your home becomes more than a place to sleep. It becomes a sanctuary. Furniture arranged for comfort rather than compromise. Lighting chosen for warmth rather than function. Rooms organized according to your habits, not shared negotiation.

Even small details matter. The temperature you prefer. The music you enjoy. The quiet you crave.

In relationships where emotional tension existed, the home often becomes a place of subtle vigilance. You learn to read the atmosphere. You anticipate moods. You adjust behavior accordingly.

When you live alone, that vigilance disappears.

The environment becomes neutral again. And neutrality is deeply restorative.

Time Without Negotiation

Perhaps the most noticeable change in single life is the transformation of time. Time becomes elastic.

You can work late without explanation. You can spend an entire afternoon reading. You can take a spontaneous trip without coordinating schedules.

There is no negotiation required.

For women accustomed to balancing their time around a partner's preferences, this freedom can initially feel unfamiliar.

But gradually it becomes normal. The calendar becomes a reflection of personal priorities rather than relational obligations.

And that shift produces something rare: spaciousness.

The Quiet Return of Curiosity

When life is no longer organized around maintaining a relationship, curiosity often returns.

Hobbies abandoned years earlier reappear. Books that were never opened are finally read. New interests develop.

This happens because emotional bandwidth expands.

Maintaining an imbalanced relationship consumes energy — often more than women realize at the time. Monitoring moods. Avoiding conflict. Providing reassurance.

When that constant expenditure stops, attention becomes available again.

And attention naturally seeks stimulation. Learning. Exploration. Creation.

The peaceful life is not static. It is quietly dynamic.

Friendship as Daily Infrastructure

Another crucial component of peaceful architecture is friendship, as discussed in Chapter 14.

Without the assumption that one partner should fulfill every emotional role, relationships diversify.

Friends become sources of laughter, advice, companionship, and shared experience.

Different friendships serve different functions. One friend for deep conversations. Another for spontaneous adventures. Another for creative collaboration.

This network creates resilience. Instead of placing all emotional expectations on a single person, connection becomes distributed. And distributed systems are stronger.

Solitude Without Isolation

There is an important distinction between solitude and isolation.

Isolation is involuntary disconnection.

Solitude is chosen space.

Women who design peaceful lives often discover they enjoy significant periods of solitude.

Not because they dislike people. But because solitude allows reflection. It provides mental quiet. It restores emotional equilibrium.

A peaceful life balances solitude and connection deliberately. Time alone to recharge. Time with others to celebrate. Neither state dominates the other.

Financial Sovereignty

Another structural element of peace is financial independence.

Money does not guarantee happiness. But financial autonomy creates safety.

When you control your resources, decisions become simpler. Housing choices are yours. Career decisions are yours. Lifestyle adjustments are yours.

There is no financial leverage attached to another person's expectations.

This autonomy reduces a specific kind of stress that many women experience in relationships: the subtle pressure to maintain economic stability through partnership.

When your livelihood is your own, that pressure disappears.

Emotional Climate Control

In shared relationships, emotional climates can shift rapidly.

One partner's stress becomes the household's stress. One partner's anxiety spreads through the environment.

Women often absorb these shifts automatically. They adjust tone, timing, and behavior to stabilize the atmosphere.

Living alone changes this dynamic entirely. Your emotional climate becomes internally regulated.

A stressful day does not escalate because someone else reacts to it.

You recover at your own pace.

The environment remains stable.

This stability is one of the most underrated aspects of peaceful living. Because nervous systems thrive in predictable environments.

The Luxury of Consistency

Consistency may sound boring. But for women who have lived inside emotionally volatile relationships, consistency feels luxurious.

Meals happen when you want them. Sleep follows your own rhythm. Weekends unfold according to your preferences.

No sudden arguments. No unpredictable tension. Just the quiet continuity of daily life.

And over time, this continuity becomes deeply restorative.

Designing a Future

Peaceful living is not merely about enjoying the present. It is also about imagining a future that aligns with your values.

Some women design futures centered around travel. Others focus on creative projects. Some invest in community work. Others cultivate gardens, businesses, art, or mentorship.

The important shift is psychological.

The future is no longer defined by relationship milestones. It is defined by personal vision.

And personal vision can evolve indefinitely.

Sovereignty as a Practice

Personal sovereignty is not a single decision. It is a practice.

Every day, you choose how your energy is allocated. You choose what enters your life. You choose what remains outside it.

This practice becomes easier over time. Boundaries become clearer. Priorities sharpen. Decisions feel less conflicted.

Because the central organizing principle is simple: peace.

The New Definition of Success

In traditional narratives, success for women has often been measured relationally. Marriage. Partnership. Family structure.

But women who design peaceful lives begin measuring success differently.

Success becomes a day that felt calm. A conversation that felt meaningful. Work that felt purposeful. Friendship that felt supportive.

This new definition is quieter. But it is also more sustainable.

Because it is grounded in lived experience rather than cultural expectation.

A Life That Fits

The architecture of a peaceful life is ultimately about fit.

Your environment fits your personality. Your schedule fits your energy. Your relationships fit your values.

Nothing is forced. Nothing is maintained purely for appearances.

Everything serves a purpose: stability, growth, joy.

And when life fits this well, the old warnings lose their power.

The fear of being alone fades. Because you are no longer alone in the way the culture predicted.

You are surrounded by the structures you built deliberately. Rituals that calm you. Spaces that support you. Relationships that nourish you.

And most importantly, a relationship with yourself that no longer requires compromise.

Peace, in the end, is not an abstract ideal. It is architecture.

And once you learn how to build it, you realize something remarkable.

You were never missing a partner. You were missing a life designed for you.

Chapter 23

Sexuality Without Negotiation

- Autonomy.

- Pleasure without negotiation.

- The freedom of choosing when and whether.

One of the quietest revolutions in a woman's life often happens in a space the culture rarely examines honestly.

Sex.

Not the theatrical version depicted in films. Not the romanticized version promised in early courtship.

But the lived, negotiated reality of sexual access within long-term relationships.

In Chapter 10 we discussed how, for generations, women have been made to feel that sexual availability is part of the implicit contract of partnership.

The details of that contract are rarely spoken directly, but the expectations hover in the background. A good female partner is attentive. She is affectionate. She does not "withhold."

The language is subtle, but the message is clear: sex is something a woman provides.

This expectation has been normalized for so long that many women do not initially recognize it as a form of obligation.

It simply feels like part of the role. Even when she is tired. Even when she is distracted. Even when desire is absent.

It puts - and men put – enormous pressure on women. You are taught to believe that to abstain means you're failing as a partner.

And when women leave relationships that carried these expectations, something surprising often happens.

They rediscover the difference between sexuality and access.

The Difference Between Desire and Availability

Sexuality is internal. It is about curiosity, attraction, sensation, imagination, pleasure.

Availability is external. It is about whether another person has access to your body.

In healthy relationships these two forces overlap naturally. Desire and availability align, and intimacy becomes mutual.

But in many long-term partnerships, the alignment gradually shifts.

Availability remains expected and desire becomes negotiable.

Women learn to say yes even when they feel neutral. Sometimes even when they feel reluctant. Not because they are coerced overtly, but because the relationship environment makes refusal uncomfortable.

A partner might become hurt. Or distant. Or defensive.

So the easiest path becomes accommodation. And accommodation slowly turns into habit.

The Cultural Silence Around Sexual Obligation

One of the most striking aspects of this dynamic is how rarely it is discussed openly.

Cultural conversations about sex tend to focus on extremes: passionate romance, scandalous affairs, or criminal coercion.

But the quieter middle ground — the space where obligation subtly replaces enthusiasm — receives far less attention.

Many women learn to navigate this terrain privately. They manage expectations. They pace themselves. They perform affection when affection feels thin.

None of this appears dramatic from the outside. But over time it can create a subtle form of fatigue.

Not because sex itself is undesirable.

But because the absence of full autonomy alters its meaning.

The Relief of Reclaiming the Body

After leaving relationships where sexual availability felt expected, many women describe a surprising sense of relief.

Not relief from sex itself. Relief from obligation.

For the first time in years, perhaps decades, their bodies belong entirely to them.

There is no expectation hovering in the background. No negotiation required. No subtle pressure to maintain another person's emotional equilibrium through physical access.

The body becomes private territory again.

And that privacy can feel deeply stabilizing.

The Myth That Single Women Are Sexually Deprived

Popular culture often frames single women — especially those living alone — as sexually deprived.

The assumption is simple: without a partner, intimacy disappears.

But this assumption misunderstands the difference between frequency and autonomy.

Sexual experiences that occur through choice, curiosity, and enthusiasm often feel richer than those that occur through routine expectation.

Some women choose periods of celibacy. Others explore dating with clearer boundaries.

Some pursue casual connections that are defined by mutual desire rather than obligation. Others discover that their relationship with their own bodies becomes more attentive and exploratory.

There is no single path.

But the defining characteristic is *freedom*.

Pleasure Without Negotiation

In relationships where sexual access is assumed, pleasure can become secondary to harmony.

Women sometimes prioritize maintaining the relationship dynamic over expressing their own preferences.

They become skilled at reading cues. Skilled at anticipating what their partner wants. Skilled at managing the emotional atmosphere of intimacy.

When obligation disappears, this dynamic changes. Pleasure becomes self-directed.

There is no need to perform enthusiasm when it is absent. There is no need to accelerate desire to meet another person's expectations.

Instead, curiosity returns. What do I actually enjoy? What pace feels natural? What conditions allow desire to appear spontaneously?

These questions can feel surprisingly new. Because many women have spent years focusing outward during intimacy.

Now the focus returns inward.

The Nervous System and Consent

Autonomy also changes how the body responds to intimacy.

The nervous system plays a central role in sexual experience.

When the body feels safe, relaxed, and unpressured, desire emerges more easily.

When the body feels obligated or monitored, tension can interfere.

Even subtle pressure can produce a low-level stress response.

This response is rarely dramatic. But it influences how the body processes sensation and desire.

When autonomy is restored, the nervous system recalibrates.

Sexual interest becomes less about meeting expectations and more about genuine curiosity.

And curiosity is fertile ground for pleasure.

Choosing When — and Whether

One of the most radical aspects of sexual autonomy is the recognition that sex is *optional*.

Not permanently optional. But situationally optional.

You can choose when it happens. You can choose *whether* it happens.

This seems obvious. But many women discover that they spent years operating under a different assumption — that sex was an ongoing responsibility within partnership.

When that assumption disappears, sexuality becomes less structured by duty.

Some women embrace periods of intense exploration. Others discover that long stretches of sexual quiet feel restorative. Neither choice is superior.

What matters is that the decision originates from personal desire rather than relational obligation.

Dating Without Automatic Access

For women who choose to date again after separation, sexual autonomy often reshapes the dating process.

Boundaries become clearer. Physical intimacy is not assumed simply because emotional connection exists.

Women who have experienced the fatigue of sexual obligation tend to move more deliberately.

They observe behavior. They notice how potential partners respond to boundaries. They evaluate whether respect and curiosity are present.

This shift changes the dynamic. Because a woman who no longer feels compelled to provide sexual access is difficult to pressure.

She is not negotiating for approval. She is assessing compatibility.

The Disappearance of Performance

Another quiet transformation occurs when sexual activity is no longer tied to maintaining a relationship.

Performance begins to fade.

Many women realize that they spent years managing the emotional reactions of their partners during intimacy.

They worried about appearing enthusiastic. They monitored whether their partner felt desired. They prioritized responsiveness.

These behaviors are understandable. But they often create a subtle distance between authentic sensation and outward performance.

When obligation disappears, authenticity becomes easier.

There is no audience to satisfy. Only experience to explore.

The Politics of Female Desire

Historically, female sexuality has been heavily regulated by cultural expectations.

Women were once expected to be passive.

Later they were encouraged to appear sexually liberated — but often within frameworks that still prioritized male pleasure.

The idea that a woman might shape her sexual life entirely around her own preferences remains surprisingly radical.

Not rejecting intimacy. Not rejecting men.

Simply deciding that access to her body requires enthusiasm.

Not tolerance. Not negotiation. Enthusiasm.

This standard quietly transforms sexual dynamics.

Because enthusiasm cannot be manufactured on demand. It appears when conditions are right.

And those conditions often include respect, safety, curiosity, and emotional ease.

Aging and Sexual Autonomy

Another misconception about single women — particularly those over forty or fifty — is that sexuality fades.

But many women report the opposite. To quote an elderly single female friend of mine, "The desire never leaves you."

As social pressure decreases and self-knowledge increases, sexual confidence often grows.

There is less concern about impressing others. Less anxiety about comparison. More willingness to communicate preferences.

Autonomy makes this possible.

Because sexual expression is no longer tethered to maintaining a partnership identity.

It becomes part of a broader exploration of pleasure, intimacy, and self-awareness.

The Freedom to Say No

Perhaps the most profound aspect of sexuality without obligation is the freedom to say *No* without consequence.

No without emotional punishment. No without guilt. No without negotiation.

This freedom transforms consent from a technical concept into a lived experience.

Consent becomes enthusiastic participation rather than reluctant agreement.

And when this standard becomes internalized, future relationships shift accordingly.

Partners who respect autonomy remain. Partners who resist it fade quickly.

Redefining Intimacy

Autonomy also expands the definition of intimacy.

Physical connection becomes one form among many. Conversation. Laughter. Shared creativity. Quiet companionship. Touch that is not sexual.

These forms of intimacy flourish when they are not overshadowed by expectation.

Sexuality becomes integrated into a broader landscape of connection rather than serving as the primary proof of relational success.

The Quiet Power of Choice

At the heart of this chapter lies a simple principle:

Choice.

Not theoretical choice. Real choice.

The ability to decide how, when, and whether your body participates in intimacy.

This choice restores something that many women did not realize had gradually eroded:

Ownership.

Ownership of time. Ownership of attention. Ownership of the body itself.

And once ownership returns, sexuality becomes less about obligation and more about exploration.

A Different Kind of Fulfillment

The cultural narrative often assumes that sexual fulfillment requires a permanent partner.

But fulfillment is more complex than proximity. It emerges from alignment.

Alignment between desire and action. Alignment between curiosity and experience. Alignment between boundaries and respect.

Women who reclaim sexual autonomy frequently discover that fulfillment has less to do with frequency and more to do with authenticity.

Sexual experiences that arise from genuine enthusiasm tend to feel richer, regardless of their frequency.

The Final Liberation

For many women, sexuality without obligation becomes one of the most liberating aspects of life after partnership.

Not because sex disappears.

But because it becomes honest.

There is no role to perform. No quota to meet. No emotional equilibrium to maintain.

Only curiosity. Only pleasure. Only choice.

And choice, in the realm of intimacy, is a form of power that transforms everything.

Because when your body belongs fully to you, every experience that follows becomes an act of willingness rather than accommodation.

Not duty. Not expectation. Just desire — when and if it arrives.

And that freedom is its own kind of peace.

Chapter 24

Money, Power, and Safety

- Economic independence as emotional protection.

- Why stability matters more than romance.

There is a quiet truth that sits beneath nearly every story about women's freedom.

Money.

Not in the glamorous sense of luxury or extravagance. Not in the cultural fantasy of wealth.

But in the simple, structural sense of autonomy.

Who pays the rent. Who controls the bank account. Who has the capacity to leave.

For centuries, women's lives were shaped by a brutal economic fact: survival required attachment to a man.

Not because women were incapable. But because the systems surrounding them were designed that way.

Women could not own property. They could not open bank accounts. They could not easily work outside the home.

Marriage was not merely romantic. It was logistical. It was economic architecture.

And that architecture created a particular kind of power imbalance.

If one person controls the resources that sustain life, the other person's freedom becomes conditional.

The Hidden Economics of Dependency
Many modern relationships no longer look overtly unequal.

Women work. Women earn. Women participate in public life.

Yet subtle forms of economic dependency still exist.

Sometimes one partner earns significantly more. Sometimes childcare responsibilities interrupt a woman's career trajectory. Sometimes financial decisions are quietly centralized in one person's hands.

None of this necessarily signals manipulation.

But it creates vulnerability.

Because the ability to leave a relationship — peacefully, safely, without chaos — depends heavily on financial stability.

This is one of the least romantic truths about independence.

Freedom requires infrastructure.

Why Financial Autonomy Changes Everything

Economic independence does not guarantee happiness. But it dramatically alters the emotional landscape of relationships.

When a woman knows she can support herself, partnership becomes *a choice rather than a necessity.*

This shift changes the tone of the relationship.

Disagreements become discussions rather than threats. Boundaries become enforceable. Respect becomes non-negotiable.

Because the unspoken leverage — the fear of financial collapse — no longer hovers in the background.

Autonomy removes the quiet pressure to tolerate what would otherwise be unacceptable.

The Stability That Money Provides

Romantic culture often portrays love as a force powerful enough to overcome practical concerns.

But stability is not an enemy of love. It is a foundation for well-being.

Stable housing. Reliable income. Control over one's schedule.

These conditions create psychological safety.

Without them, emotional life becomes fragile. Arguments feel riskier. Uncertainty becomes exhausting. Decision-making becomes clouded by fear.

When financial stability exists independently of a relationship, the nervous system relaxes.

Choices become clearer.

Not because money solves every problem. But because it removes the constant background anxiety of survival.

The Cost of Romantic Idealism

Many women were raised with the belief that emotional connection should take priority over financial pragmatism. Love conquers all. Follow your heart. Money is secondary.

These phrases sound noble. But they often obscure a crucial reality: economic stability profoundly shapes quality of life.

Rent must be paid. Food must be purchased. Healthcare must be accessed. Transportation must function.

When these basic needs are unstable, romantic relationships absorb enormous strain.

Arguments about money become arguments about security. And insecurity erodes intimacy quickly.

Why Stability Matters More Than Romance

Romance is exhilarating.

It produces intensity. It creates emotional highs.

But stability produces something deeper. Peace.

A stable life allows for routine. Predictability. Long-term planning. Health. Friendship. Creative work.

These elements rarely appear in romantic narratives, yet they shape daily experience far more than grand gestures.

When women evaluate relationships through the lens of stability rather than romance alone, priorities shift.

A partner's reliability becomes more meaningful than their charm. Financial responsibility becomes more significant than dramatic affection.

Because reliability protects the future. Charm does not.

Economic Abuse: The Unspoken Reality

In some relationships, financial dynamics move beyond imbalance into control.

Economic abuse is a form of manipulation that receives far less public attention than other forms of mistreatment.

It can include:
Restricting access to shared money.
Monitoring spending excessively.
Preventing a partner from working.
Accumulating debt in another person's name.
Withholding resources as punishment.

These behaviors are not merely financial. They are psychological. They are controlling.

They create dependency. And dependency makes leaving extraordinarily difficult.

Women who regain financial autonomy after experiencing economic control often describe the moment as transformative.

Not because wealth appears. But because choice returns.

The Link Between Money and Safety

Safety is not only physical. It is also logistical.

A safe life includes: The ability to secure housing. The ability to move locations if necessary. The ability to access legal support. The ability to provide for children.

These capacities require resources.

When women lack financial autonomy, safety can become compromised. Not because every relationship is dangerous. But because leaving unsafe situations becomes complicated.

Economic independence reduces that vulnerability. It provides exit routes. And exit routes create leverage.

The Psychological Power of Self-Provision

There is also a psychological dimension to financial independence.

When a woman supports herself, her sense of competence strengthens.

She learns that she can manage complexity. She learns that uncertainty can be navigated. She learns that stability can be built deliberately.

This self-trust becomes powerful. Because it reduces the temptation to remain in relationships out of fear. Fear of bills. Fear of housing instability. Fear of being unable to cope alone.

When these fears dissolve, the emotional calculus of relationships changes dramatically.

The Myth of the Financially "Taken Care Of" Woman

Another cultural narrative suggests that being financially supported by a partner represents security.

At first glance, this can appear appealing. Less stress. More comfort.

But reliance on another person's income carries risk. Not because support is inherently harmful. But because circumstances change. Jobs disappear. Relationships shift. Health crises occur. Divorce happens. Widowhood happens.

If a woman has not maintained her own financial literacy and earning capacity, these transitions can be devastating.

Economic independence is not about rejecting partnership.

It is about preserving resilience.

The Quiet Strength of Modest Stability

Financial autonomy does not require extraordinary wealth.

Many women discover that modest stability — consistent income, manageable expenses, a small savings buffer — provides profound peace.

The goal is not luxury. The goal is *sovereignty*. Being able to pay your own rent. Being able to make decisions without financial coercion. Being able to walk away from situations that compromise dignity.

These conditions produce emotional safety. And emotional safety is the foundation of a peaceful life.

Rethinking Success

For many women raised in romantic cultures, success was once measured by partnership: Marriage. A shared home. A shared life.

But as women reclaim financial independence, success begins to look different.

Success might mean: Owning a small apartment. Building retirement savings. Running a small business. Maintaining a stable job that allows freedom and flexibility.

These achievements rarely appear in fairy tales. Yet they provide the structure that makes autonomy sustainable.

Why Independence Strengthens Relationships

Interestingly, financial independence does not weaken healthy relationships. It strengthens them.

When two people enter a partnership without economic dependency, the relationship becomes more balanced.

Neither partner is trapped. Both remain because they choose to.

This dynamic fosters mutual respect. Disagreements can occur without threatening survival. Both individuals maintain personal agency.

In this environment, intimacy becomes genuine rather than transactional.

The Intersection of Money and Time

Financial stability also protects something equally valuable. Time.

When resources are secure, time can be allocated intentionally. Time for rest. Time for friendships. Time for learning new skills. Time for reflection.

In unstable financial environments, time becomes consumed by urgency. Extra work hours. Constant budgeting anxiety. Emergency problem-solving. Economic independence creates breathing room.

And breathing room allows life to expand beyond survival.

The Role of Financial Literacy

Economic autonomy also requires knowledge.

Understanding budgeting. Understanding debt. Understanding investing and retirement planning.

For generations, women were excluded from these conversations. Financial decisions were often handled by husbands or fathers.

As a result, many women enter adulthood without the confidence to manage complex financial systems.

Learning these skills can feel intimidating at first. But financial literacy is learnable.

And once acquired, it becomes a powerful form of protection.

Because knowledge prevents manipulation.

Teaching the Next Generation

The relationship between women and money is evolving rapidly.

Younger generations are increasingly encouraged to pursue education, careers, and financial independence.

But cultural messages about romance still compete with these lessons.

Young women are often told they can "have it all." Career, partnership, family, stability.

Sometimes they can. Sometimes the balancing act becomes exhausting.

Teaching financial independence early ensures that regardless of relationship outcomes, autonomy remains intact.

When Romance Meets Reality

There is nothing wrong with love. There is nothing wrong with partnership.

Human beings are relational creatures. Connection enriches life.

But connection cannot replace infrastructure. Love does not pay rent. Affection does not cover medical bills. Compatibility does not replace retirement planning.

When romance is grounded in financial stability, relationships become more resilient.

When romance replaces stability, relationships become fragile.

The Freedom to Walk Away

Ultimately, the most profound gift of economic independence is the ability to leave.

Not because leaving is always desirable. But because the option exists.

Knowing that you can walk away changes how you tolerate behavior. It strengthens boundaries. It clarifies values.

And it prevents the quiet desperation that emerges when someone feels financially trapped.

Freedom is not defined by constant movement. It is defined by the absence of confinement.

Building a Life That Cannot Be Taken Away

At the heart of this chapter lies a simple philosophy: *Build a life that does not depend entirely on another person's goodwill.*

This does not mean rejecting love. It means constructing stability first. Income. Housing. Savings. Skills. Community.

These elements create a structure that cannot easily be dismantled by relationship changes.

When this structure exists, partnership becomes an addition rather than a foundation.

And additions can be joyful. Because they are not carrying the entire weight of survival.

The Quiet Power of Financial Peace

Many women who achieve financial independence describe a moment of realization.

Bills are paid. Savings exist. The household runs smoothly.

And suddenly they recognize something subtle but profound: They are safe.

Not invincible. But secure enough to breathe. Secure enough to make decisions without fear. Secure enough to design a life intentionally.

That quiet sense of safety is not dramatic. It does not appear in romantic movies.

But it transforms daily existence. Because when survival is stable, everything else becomes possible.

The Real Meaning of Power

Power is often misunderstood.

It is not domination. It is not control over others.

Real power is the ability to protect your own well-being.

Economic independence provides that protection. It shields dignity. It supports autonomy. It prevents exploitation.

And it ensures that relationships remain voluntary.

When a woman controls the resources that sustain her life, she does not need to tolerate disrespect in exchange for security.

She can walk away. She can rebuild. She can begin again.

The Foundation of Peace
In the end, money itself is not the goal.

Peace is.

But peace requires stability. And stability requires resources.

Economic independence is not about greed. It is about safety.

It is about ensuring that no relationship — no matter how emotionally complicated — holds the power to destabilize your entire life.

When that foundation exists, love becomes freer. Choices become clearer.

And the future becomes something you shape rather than something you fear.

Because a life built on your own economic footing cannot easily be taken from you.

And that security, more than romance, is what makes peace possible.

Chapter 25

Community, Creativity, and Contribution

- Purpose beyond partnership.

- Building legacy without marriage.

There is a moment that arrives quietly in the life of a woman who has stepped outside the gravitational pull of romantic expectation.

It often arrives after the noise has faded. After the arguments about whether leaving was selfish. After the anxious nights when conditioning tried to lure her back. After the slow construction of stability.

The moment arrives when she looks around her life and notices something surprising: *Space.*

Not emptiness. Space.

Space where obligation used to sit. Space where appeasement once lived. Space where emotional labor once quietly drained her attention.

And for the first time, she realizes a question she was never encouraged to ask.

If my life is not organized around maintaining a relationship, what *can* it be organized around?

This is the question that opens the final stage of the awakening. Because when partnership stops being the central axis of identity, something else has room to emerge: *Purpose.*

The Lie That Partnership Is the Center of Life

For centuries, women were told that the central project of their lives was partnership.

Find a man. Keep him. Build a household around him. Support his ambitions. Raise children. Maintain the emotional climate.

Every other aspiration was positioned as secondary. Creative pursuits were hobbies. Friendships were accessories. Personal development was indulgent.

The relationship was the main event. Everything else existed in its shadow.

This cultural structure did not merely shape relationships. It shaped time. It shaped identity. It shaped the allocation of energy.

And when women step outside this structure, the shift can feel disorienting at first.

Because suddenly, the organizing principle disappears.

The Terrifying Freedom of an Unstructured Life

When partnership is no longer the anchor of life, the horizon widens.

This widening can feel exhilarating.

It can also feel unsettling. Because the absence of obligation requires the presence of choice.

Choice about how to spend your days. Choice about what matters. Choice about where your energy goes.

Many women initially experience this freedom as uncertainty: What am I supposed to do with my life now?

The question itself reveals how deeply the cultural script ran.

Because men are rarely asked this question in the same way. Men have historically been encouraged to build identities around work, craft, philosophy, invention, and leadership.

Women were encouraged to build identities around relationships.

So when relationships stop defining the structure of life, the terrain must be rediscovered.

And rediscovery is both thrilling and frightening.

Purpose Is Not One Thing

One of the first misconceptions women encounter in this stage is the idea that purpose must be grand. A world-changing career. A major creative achievement. A public contribution.

But purpose does not have to be monumental.

Purpose is simply the direction of meaningful attention.

It is what you care about enough to invest time in.

For some women, that may indeed be professional achievement. For others, it may be art. Or activism. Or mentorship. Or gardening. Or community building. Or learning.

Purpose is not defined by scale. It is defined by sincerity.

And when women stop pouring enormous amounts of energy into maintaining relationships that require constant emotional management, that sincerity has room to flourish.

Creativity: The Forgotten Dimension of Female Life

One of the most striking transformations that occurs after women reclaim their time is the return of creativity.

Creativity is not limited to painting or writing. It includes problem-solving. Design. Storytelling. Cooking. Teaching. Building new systems.

For many women, creativity was quietly suppressed by the demands of relationship maintenance. Not intentionally. But structurally.

Creative work requires concentration. Mental space. Long stretches of uninterrupted time.

Yet emotional labor fragments attention.

Constant monitoring of another person's moods. Managing schedules. Resolving small conflicts. Anticipating needs.

These tasks consume cognitive energy.

When that energy is reclaimed, creativity reappears. Often suddenly. Often intensely.

Women who had not written in years begin writing again.

Women who abandoned artistic pursuits rediscover them.

Women who never thought of themselves as creative realize that their minds had simply been occupied elsewhere.

Creativity does not disappear. It waits.

Contribution: The Desire to Give

Human beings possess a deep instinct to contribute. To participate in something larger than themselves.

Partnership has often been presented as the primary vehicle for this instinct. Build a family. Support a partner. Raise children.

But contribution can take many forms. Mentorship. Volunteer work. Community organizing. Professional excellence. Creative output that inspires others. Support networks among friends. Intergenerational relationships.

These forms of contribution often become more visible when the structure of life expands beyond coupledom.

Women begin to see how many avenues for impact exist. And they begin to choose intentionally.

Community: The Overlooked Structure

One of the quiet tragedies of modern romantic culture is how it isolates people.

The couple becomes the central unit. Social life shrinks around that pair. Friendships are deprioritized. Extended community weakens.

When a relationship ends, many women initially fear that they will become socially isolated.

But the opposite often occurs.

Freed from the demands of couple-centered living, they begin rebuilding broader networks. Friendships deepen. New communities emerge.

Shared interests bring people together. Book clubs. Creative workshops. Volunteer organizations. Neighborhood networks. Professional collaborations.

These communities provide something profoundly different from romantic partnerships. Mutual support without ownership. Connection without possession. Belonging without hierarchy.

Interdependence Without Possession

Healthy communities operate on a principle distinct from romantic exclusivity: Interdependence.

People support each other. But they do not claim each other.

They offer help. But they do not demand emotional monopoly.

They share time. But they do not expect constant prioritization.

This structure allows relationships to remain flexible and resilient. If one connection changes, the entire network does not collapse.

This is one reason why women who cultivate rich community networks often experience greater life satisfaction than those whose social world revolves around a single partner.

Community distributes emotional support across many relationships.

And distributed support is far more stable.

The Myth of the Married Legacy

Another narrative that shapes women's lives is the belief that legacy requires marriage and children. That without these structures, life lacks lasting meaning.

But history tells a different story.

Many individuals who shaped culture, science, art, and philosophy did so outside traditional family structures.

Legacy is not limited to genetic continuation. It can take many forms. Ideas. Art. Institutions. Mentorship. Acts of courage that ripple outward through communities.

Even small acts of generosity can alter the trajectory of another person's life.

Legacy is influence. And influence is not confined to marriage.

The Creative Freedom of Solitude

Solitude provides something rare in modern life: Deep thinking.

When the mind is not constantly negotiating relational dynamics, it begins exploring more expansive questions.

What interests me? What do I want to learn? What problems do I want to solve?

This mental freedom often leads women into unexpected intellectual territories. History. Philosophy. Science. Politics. Creative expression. New skills.

Solitude becomes fertile ground for exploration. And exploration fuels contribution.

Designing a Life of Meaning

Once women realize that partnership is optional rather than obligatory, the design of life becomes a deliberate act.

Time becomes a canvas. What fills it becomes a matter of values.

Some women prioritize travel. Others pursue education. Others build businesses. Others dedicate themselves to activism. Others cultivate quiet lives centered around art, nature, and friendship.

There is no single correct structure.

The power lies in the freedom to choose.

The Richness of Female Collaboration

Another dimension of post-partnership life often surprises women: Collaboration with other women.

When competition for male attention disappears, cooperation expands.

Women share ideas. Support each other's projects. Build networks of mutual encouragement.

Historically, women's collaboration has produced remarkable outcomes. Social movements. Educational institutions. Charitable organizations. Creative collectives.

These collaborations flourish when women stop viewing each other as rivals within a romantic marketplace.

Instead, they become allies within a shared project of building meaningful lives.

Contribution as a Source of Joy

One of the most unexpected discoveries many women make is that contribution generates profound satisfaction.

Helping someone learn a skill. Supporting a friend through difficulty. Creating something beautiful. Organizing a community initiative.

These experiences create a sense of purpose that differs from romantic validation.

They are quieter. But they are deeper. Because they connect the individual to something larger than personal status.

They transform life from a performance into a participation.

The Freedom to Grow

Another advantage of a life not organized around maintaining partnership is the freedom to evolve.

People change. Interests shift. Careers transform. Geography moves.

When identity is tied too tightly to a relationship, these changes become disruptive.

But when identity rests on personal purpose and community contribution, change becomes natural.

Growth is expected. Exploration is encouraged. The self remains fluid.

Redefining Fulfillment

For many women raised within romantic narratives, fulfillment was once imagined as a stable partnership accompanied by social approval.

But fulfillment can take many shapes.

A studio filled with creative work. A community garden that feeds neighbors. A mentoring program that supports young women. A body of writing that sparks conversations. A quiet home filled with books and meaningful friendships.

Fulfillment is not a standardized product. It is an ecosystem of experiences that align with personal values.

Choosing to Opt Out: The Radical Art of Doing Nothing

It is also perfectly acceptable to opt out of constant participation. Not every meaningful life requires a committee, a cause, or a calendar full of community meetings.

Sometimes the most honest contribution a person can make is simply living quietly and well.

A peaceful life does not always look productive from the outside.

Sometimes it looks like doing very little at all, and discovering that very little is, in fact, more than enough.

The Terrible Fate of Sitting on a Porch With a Cat

There is a quiet kind of luxury in enjoying the peace of your own company.

Not the forced independence people assume when they hear the word *alone*, but the calm pleasure of inhabiting your own life without constant negotiation.

You make tea when you want tea. You sit where the sun falls. You think your thoughts all the way through without interruption.

The world slows down. Solitude stops feeling like absence and starts feeling like space.

People often treat this as suspicious, as though contentment without an audience must be temporary.

But the truth is simpler: some of us genuinely like the person we are when no one else is directing the atmosphere.

In our own company we become quieter, clearer, less defensive. The nervous system settles. The day belongs to us.

To enjoy solitude is not to reject other people.

It is simply to refuse the idea that life must always be shared to be meaningful.

Sometimes the richest companionship available is the one you have with yourself — a conversation that requires no explanation, no performance, and no permission.

I am a contented non-joiner of things. And I unashamedly say that I love my own company.

I have a further confession: I am often at my happiest sitting on my porch, with my laptop, watching the small dramas of the natural world unfold — birds in the bird bath, clouds rearranging themselves with theatrical laziness — with my cat (yes, cat) stretched beside me like a furry supervisor of stillness.

The Quiet Power of a Life Well Lived

When women construct lives rich with community, creativity, and contribution, something remarkable happens.

The cultural threat that once hovered over them loses its power.

"You'll die alone."

The phrase sounds absurd in the context of a life full of meaningful relationships and purposeful activity.

Because "alone" was never the correct word.

What these women built was not isolation. It was independence within connection.

Building a Legacy That Reflects You

Legacy is not measured by how closely one's life followed a cultural script.

It is measured by the authenticity of the life lived. The ideas shared. The people supported. The projects created. The courage demonstrated.

Women who step outside traditional expectations often discover that they have far more capacity for influence than they imagined.

Because their time is no longer consumed by maintaining structures that do not nourish them.

Instead, that time fuels creativity. Contribution. Community.

The Expansion of Life

Perhaps the most profound transformation of all is this: Life expands.

When emotional labor is no longer draining constant energy...

When partnership is no longer the organizing center...

When autonomy stabilizes the foundation of daily living...

The horizon widens.

New interests appear. New friendships form. New ideas take shape.

And the woman who once feared the label of "alone" discovers that her life has become larger than she ever expected.

Not smaller. Larger.

The Final Truth About Purpose

Purpose does not arrive from external validation.

It grows from engagement. From curiosity. From participation in the world.

And women who step outside the narrow expectation that their lives must revolve around partnership often discover something quietly revolutionary.

Their capacity for meaning was never dependent on being chosen.

It was always waiting for them to choose.

What to build. What to share. What to contribute.

And once that choice is made, life becomes not an absence of relationship... but an abundance of possibility.

The next chapter will carry this realization to its final destination.

Because when a woman builds a life rooted in autonomy, community, creativity, and contribution, the last cultural threat loses its sting.

The phrase that was meant to frighten her becomes something else entirely.

A declaration. A shrug.

Liberation.

Die alone, then.

And finally... she understands why that was never a threat at all.

Chapter 26

Die Alone, Then

- The phrase, reclaimed.

- Why peace is not loneliness.

- Why fear was the real prison.

- A manifesto for the unapologetic woman.

- Alone, not lonely

There is a sentence that has followed women for generations.

It is delivered casually. Sometimes jokingly. Sometimes with a hint of pity. Sometimes with open hostility.

But always with the same intention. To frighten.

"You'll die alone."

The phrase is rarely spoken to men with the same weight.

For men, solitude is often interpreted as independence, eccentricity, even freedom.

For women, it is framed as failure. A warning. A prophecy. A punishment.

The message behind the sentence is simple: Without a man, your life will end in emptiness. Without a man, you will be abandoned by the world. Without a man, your existence will shrink into silence.

For centuries, this fear has worked.

It has rushed women into relationships that did not nourish them. It has kept them inside marriages that drained them. It has convinced them to endure loneliness inside partnership rather than risk solitude outside it.

Because the threat was not merely about death. It was about humiliation.

The humiliation of having lived a life that did not conform.

But something strange happens when a woman stops fearing the sentence.

When she looks at the warning and answers calmly:

"Die alone, then."

Not as surrender. As refusal.

The Power of the Threat
Fear has always been the most efficient tool of social control.

Not force. Not violence.

Fear.

Fear persuades people to regulate themselves. Fear persuades them to accept conditions they might otherwise question. Fear persuades them to remain inside systems that do not serve them.

For women, one of the most powerful fears cultivated across generations has been the fear of isolation.

From childhood, girls are taught that connection is their greatest currency.

Be liked. Be desirable. Be chosen.

Do not be too difficult. Do not be too independent. Do not risk rejection.

Because rejection, in this narrative, leads to abandonment.

And abandonment leads to the ultimate catastrophe.

Being alone.

This conditioning begins early. Fairy tales end in marriage. Romantic comedies end in reconciliation. Family conversations center around relationships.

Even compliments reinforce the script: "You'll make someone very happy one day."

The assumption behind all of this messaging is clear: A woman's life reaches completion through partnership.

And without it, something essential is missing.

The Hidden Loneliness of Conformity

Yet the irony of this fear is rarely acknowledged.

Many women who followed the script precisely are not free from loneliness.

Loneliness exists inside marriages. Inside relationships. Inside homes filled with people.

Loneliness is not simply the absence of company.

It is the absence of recognition. The absence of emotional reciprocity. The absence of being seen.

Many women experience this form of loneliness while technically partnered.

They lie beside someone who does not truly know them. They perform emotional labor that is rarely acknowledged. They maintain harmony while quietly shrinking. They adapt themselves so thoroughly to the expectations of others that their own voice fades.

And the world congratulates them for their success.

Because the appearance of partnership matters more, culturally, than the quality of the life inside it.

Peace Is Not Loneliness

This book has argued a simple but disruptive idea.

Peace is not loneliness.

Peace is the absence of unnecessary conflict. Peace is the absence of constant emotional negotiation. Peace is the freedom to exist without performing. Peace is waking up without anticipating someone else's mood. Peace is speaking without calculating the emotional consequences. Peace is living inside your own mind without interference.

For women who have spent years regulating another person's emotional weather, this peace can feel unfamiliar at first.

Silence replaces tension. Calm replaces vigilance.

The body slowly learns that it no longer needs to anticipate the next emotional shift.

And what initially feels like emptiness begins to reveal itself as spaciousness. Space to think. Space to create. Space to breathe.

The Real Prison Was Fear

When women finally step outside the fear of being alone, a realization often arrives with startling clarity.

The prison was never solitude.

The prison was fear.

Fear of social judgment. Fear of aging without validation. Fear of disappointing family expectations. Fear of making the wrong choice. Fear of being the woman people whisper about.

Fear of the phrase that had hovered over them for decades:

"You'll die alone."

Fear kept women negotiating away their peace. Fear kept them apologizing for their boundaries. Fear kept them tolerating dynamics that drained them.

But once fear loosens its grip, the landscape changes.

Because the threat loses its power.

Reclaiming the Phrase

To reclaim a threat is to neutralize it.

Language loses its ability to control when its emotional charge dissolves.

"Die alone, then."

The phrase no longer sounds tragic when spoken by a woman who has built a life she values.

It sounds calm. Even defiant.

Because the implication behind the original warning—that a life without male partnership is inherently empty—has been proven false.

A woman can build a life filled with friendship, creativity, contribution, and joy.

She can experience love in many forms.

She can support others and be supported in return.

She can live with dignity, autonomy, and meaning.

And when she reaches the end of that life, she will not be measuring its worth by whether it matched a cultural script.

She will measure it by whether it was authentically hers.

Alone Is Not the Same as Lonely

One of the most persistent confusions in modern culture is the conflation of solitude with loneliness.

They are not the same.

Loneliness is emotional disconnection.

Solitude is physical independence.

A person can be lonely in a crowded room.

And a person can feel deeply connected while living alone.

Women who cultivate rich friendships, community networks, and meaningful work rarely experience the isolation that cultural warnings predict. Instead, they experience a form of connection that is more diverse and resilient than the single-channel intimacy of romantic partnership.

Friendships provide emotional reciprocity. Communities provide belonging. Creative pursuits provide expression. Contribution provides purpose.

These structures create a life that is interconnected without being dependent on one central relationship.

The Unapologetic Woman

There is a particular kind of woman who emerges at the end of this process.

She is not bitter. She is not hostile. She is not trying to prove anything.

She is simply done apologizing. She does not apologize for her independence. She does not apologise for being single. She does not apologize for choosing peace.

She does not apologize for declining relationships that require self-erasure. She does not apologize for aging without panic. She does not apologize for building a life that does not revolve around romantic partnership.

Her existence is calm.

But it is also quietly revolutionary.

Because she demonstrates something that many systems depend on women never discovering.

That a woman can be complete on her own.

A Manifesto for the Unapologetic Woman

Let this chapter end not with a warning, but with a declaration.

A manifesto for the woman who refuses the old scripts.

You are not incomplete.

You were never waiting for someone to finish you.

You are not behind.

Life is not a race toward partnership.

You are not difficult for wanting peace. You are discerning.

You are not selfish for protecting your time and energy. You are responsible for your life.

You are not unlovable because you refuse relationships that require self-erasure. You are self-respecting.

You are not failing because you choose solitude over dysfunction. You are choosing health.

And you are not tragic if your life unfolds outside the traditional narrative.

You are simply free.

The Quiet Courage of Choosing Yourself
Choosing yourself is not a single decision.

It is a series of decisions. Small ones. Daily ones.

Saying no when a situation drains you.

Leaving when a relationship diminishes you.

Prioritizing your well-being over social approval.

Building friendships that nourish you.

Pursuing work that excites you.

Protecting the quiet spaces where your identity grows.

Each of these decisions strengthens autonomy. Each of them weakens the old fear.

And over time, the woman who once worried about being alone becomes someone who understands the value of her own company.

The Life That Opens
When women release the fear of dying alone, something unexpected happens.

Life becomes more vivid.

Not smaller. Larger.

Because decisions are no longer made from panic. They are made from curiosity. From alignment. From genuine desire.

Some women will still choose partnership. But they will choose it freely.

Not because they are afraid of solitudeBut because the relationship genuinely enhances their lives.

Others will remain single and build rich networks of friendship, creativity, and contribution.

Both paths become equally valid.

The difference is that neither is driven by fear.

The Final Reframing

Every culture creates stories that shape behavior.

For generations, the story told to women was simple: Without partnership, you will be alone. Without partnership, you will be unhappy. Without partnership, your life will lack meaning.

But this story collapses when women begin telling their own.

Stories of autonomy. Stories of friendship. Stories of creative fulfillment. Stories of peace. Stories of lives that were not defined by romantic status but by authenticity.

When enough women live these stories, the warning loses its credibility.

"You'll die alone."

The phrase stops functioning as a threat.

It becomes an empty relic of a narrative that no longer holds power.

And If You Do?

Let us address the sentence directly.

What if, at the end of your life, you are physically alone?

What if there is no spouse sitting beside your bed?

What if your final moments are quiet?

Will that erase the decades of experiences you lived? The friendships you nurtured? The work you created? The people you helped? The joy you experienced?

Of course not.

Death is a moment.

Life is everything that happens before it.

And a life lived with authenticity, peace, and self-respect cannot be diminished by the circumstances of its final hour.

Die Alone, Then

So let us return to the phrase.

"Die alone, then."

Once spoken as a threat.

Now spoken as freedom.

It no longer means abandonment. It means independence. It means living without coercion. It means refusing relationships that require self-erasure. It means trusting that a meaningful life can take many forms.

And it means understanding something that many systems worked hard to conceal.

That a woman's peace is not something she must trade for love.

It is something she can build for herself.

Alone, Not Lonely

At the end of this journey, the woman who once feared solitude often discovers something unexpected.

She is not alone.

She is surrounded by the life she built. Friends who know her deeply. Communities that value her presence. Creative work that expresses her voice. Experiences that reflect her curiosity. Memories that belong entirely to her.

And perhaps most importantly, she has something she never had when fear controlled her choices.

A relationship with herself that is grounded in trust.

The Last Word

This book began with a warning that has haunted women for generations.

"You'll die alone."

It ends with a different understanding.

A woman who lives according to her own values, who protects her peace, who builds meaningful connections and contributions, does not fear that sentence.

Because she knows something the culture once tried to hide.

Alone is not the opposite of love.

Loneliness is not the price of independence.

And peace is not a consolation prize for women who failed to find partnership.

Peace is the reward for women who chose themselves.

And if the world still whispers the warning... Let it.

You already know the answer.

Die alone, then.

Afterword

Die Alone, Then

If you have read this far, you have likely already sensed the quiet truth beneath the noise: the fear of being alone was never really about solitude.

It was about control.

For generations women were warned that the worst possible ending was independence without a man beside them.

The phrase *"you'll die alone"* was delivered like a prophecy, a threat, a moral correction for daring to step outside the script. It was meant to keep women negotiating, accommodating, shrinking, and enduring.

But the longer you examine that warning, the stranger it becomes.

Everyone dies alone.

Not because we are abandoned, but because the final crossing is an individual experience. Partners cannot walk through it for us. Families cannot stand in our place. The moment belongs to the self.

And yet only women are taught to fear it.

This book was never a declaration that partnership is worthless. Many women build beautiful lives with loving partners.

The point is simpler and far more radical: partnership must be a choice, not a survival strategy.

A woman who stays because she *wants to* is free.

A woman who stays because she *fears being alone* is negotiating under pressure.

What changes everything is the moment that pressure dissolves.

When a woman understands that solitude is not failure...
When she recognises that peace is not emptiness...
When she experiences the relief of living without constant emotional management...

Something shifts.

She stops bargaining with her own life.

She begins making decisions from clarity rather than fear.

Some women will still choose partnership, but they will choose it differently — calmly, deliberately, with standards that cannot be bullied down by the ticking clock of cultural anxiety.

Others will discover that the quiet life they were warned about is not tragic at all.

It is spacious. It is self-directed. It is full of friendships, ideas, projects, laughter, and the deep satisfaction of inhabiting one's own mind without apology.

And sometimes, yes, it involves a porch, a notebook, and a cat.

The point is not whether you marry, separate, date, or remain single.

The point is that the decision belongs to you.

So if someone leans forward one day and says the old line — the one meant to terrify women back into obedience — you may find yourself smiling.

"You'll die alone."

Perhaps.

But you will live free.

And that is the part they were always afraid you would discover.

This unapologetic non-fiction guide for women reveals the hidden worlds, habits, histories, and emotional architectures many men keep tucked away. It aims to empower women, rather than breed suspicion or resentment.

The Secret Lives of Men will give you the tools to see clearly, demand honesty, set boundaries, and reclaim your emotional power.

No compromises. No excuses. No apologies.

This is not a war on men, nor a work on the psychology of men. It's about the impact of men's secrets on women. It's a wake-up call for women tired of making excuses, feeling hurt, absorbing the fallout, and rationalizing patterns that undermine their lives.

It's time to stop paying the price for male secrecy—and start living on your terms.

You loved him. You were generous with your time, your attention, and your body. Intimacy felt natural—part of the connection you were building together.

But slowly, something changed.

Sex became reassurance. Affection became maintenance.

And the relationship you once entered with desire began to feel like something you had to manage.

The fear beneath it all: *If I don't perform, I'll be replaced.*

In The Resentment Years: When Desire Becomes Duty, Mina V. Adler explores the quiet transformation many women experience in long relationships or marriages: the moment when love turns into labor and intimacy begins to feel like obligation.

With sharp psychological insight and uncompromising honesty. Adler exposes the invisible expectations that shape modern relationships -especially the subtle pressure many women feel to maintain order and keep their man.

When did desire become duty?

www.ingramcontent.com/pod-product-compliance
Lightning Source LLC
Chambersburg PA
CBHW051434050726
47593CB00005B/1786